THE LAMB OF GOD

*The Bible's Unfolding Revelation of
Sacrifice*

*A Devotional, Biblical / Theological
Study in Soteriology*

Robert L. Reymond

MENTOR

Copyright © Robert L. Reymond 2006

ISBN 1-84550-181-0
ISBN 978-1-84550-181-5

10 9 8 7 6 5 4 3 2 1

Published in 2006
in the Mentor Imprint
by
Christian Focus Publications, Ltd.,
Geanies House, Fearn, Ross-shire,
IV20 1TW, Scotland, UK

www.christianfocus.com

Cover design by Danie Van Straaten

Printed and bound in Scotland
by Bell & Bain

CONTENTS

PREFACE 5

1. INTRODUCTION 7

2. THE LAMB PROPHESIED: GENESIS 3:15, 21 11

3. THE LAMB SYMBOLIZED: GENESIS 22:1-14 17

4. THE LAMB TYPIFIED: EXODUS 12:1-13 23

5. THE LAMB SIGNIFIED: EXODUS 25–40; LEVITICUS 8–9 27

6. THE LAMB CODIFIED: LEVITICUS 1–7; 16:1-16 37

7. THE LAMB DEIFIED: ISAIAH 7:14-16; 9:6-7 43

8. THE LAMB PERSONIFIED: ISAIAH 52:13–53:12 69

9. THE LAMB IDENTIFIED: JOHN 1:29, 35 81

10. THE LAMB CRUCIFIED: THE FOUR GOSPELS 89

11. THE LAMB CLARIFIED: THE NEW TESTAMENT LETTERS 93

12. THE LAMB GLORIFIED: JOHN'S REVELATION 103

13. CONCLUSION 109

PREFACE

This monograph evolved over the years from a sermon series that I preached in the 1980s in the Concord Presbyterian Church in Waterloo, Illinois, to a study I prepared for my students in a hermeneutics course at Knox Theological Seminary to illustrate the unity of the Old and New Testaments that I entitled 'The Bible's Unfolding Revelation of Its "Lamb of God" Teaching: A Devotional Biblical-Theological Study in Soteriology,' and finally to the form in which it appears here that I have entitled *The Lamb of God*

This is not a day to play around with or to endorse theological novelties. Most if not all new ideas today in the field of soteriology are highly suspect, if not heretical, as in the cases of the so-called 'New Perspective on Paul' and the Auburn Avenue Vision, each of which calls into question in its own way the Reformed doctrine of justification by faith alone that is the heart and core of the biblical gospel. So I will not take offense if scholars who read this monograph should determine that it does not break new theological ground. Indeed, I hope they will so determine. About a critic who had concluded that his view of Scripture took his readers back to the pre-critical seventeenth century, I heard Francis Schaeffer say that he was disappointed: 'I had hoped that it took them back to the first.' This expresses my sentiment about what I write here about Christ's 'Lamb work'.

I hope, in this day when Christ's vicarious atonement and penal substitution as God's remedy for human sin are being denied on all sides, that it will prove useful in making the biblical case once again that the death of Jesus of Nazareth, the incarnate Son of God and God's Messiah, was 'Lamb work', that is, *sacrificial* work in the stead of sinners that was progressively revealed in the Old Testament and fulfilled and clarified in the New.

Robert L. Reymond

July 2006

CHAPTER ONE

INTRODUCTION

The central theme of Holy Scripture is the unfolding revelation of its doctrinal teaching on Jesus as the 'slain Lamb of God'. If it may be said of any other doctrine that it runs like a cord through Scripture, it is not an overstatement to say that the doctrine of Jesus as God's slain Lamb runs like a thick cable from Genesis to Revelation binding the entirety of Scripture together. Indeed, Revelation 13:8 speaks of Jesus as the 'Lamb that was slain *from* [*apo*] the creation of the world'[1] while 1 Peter 1:19-20 speaks of the 'precious blood of Christ, a lamb without blemish or defect [who] was chosen *before* [*pro*] the creation of the world'. So the 'Lamb of God' doctrine is ultimately rooted (as is every other doctrine) in the divine decree. The following verses attest to this fact:

Luke 22:12: '...the Son of Man is going [to the cross] in accordance with the decree [*kata to horismenon*].'

Acts 2:23: '[Jesus], by the determining purpose [*tē horismenē boulē*] and foreknowledge [*prognōsei*] of God, was handed over, [and] you with wicked hands put him to death by nailing him to the cross.'

Acts 4:24-28: In this passage the entire early church confessed to God that Herod and Pontius Pilate, with the Gentiles and leaders of Israel,

---

[1]The Lamb was slain from the creation of the world in the sense that the death of Christ was decreed from all eternity. The RSV and the NASV under the influence of Revelation 17:8, place the phrase 'from the creation of the world' in Revelation 13:8 with the verb 'written' rather than with the verb 'slain'. But it is unlikely that this phrase that is placed immediately after the verb 'slain' in the original Greek should be detached from the verb immediately preceding it and attached to the verb 'written' that is separated from this phrase by twelve words.

did to Jesus 'what your hand and your will [*boulē*] predestined [*proōrisen*] should happen'.

Ephesians 3:11: Here we are informed that God's 'eternal purpose … [he] accomplished in the Christ, Jesus our Lord'.

Hebrews 13:20: This verse speaks not only about the 'eternal covenant' but also about 'the blood' of the eternal covenant. Clearly the sacrificial death of Jesus Christ was a central element within the eternal covenant of redemption.

It is not my intention in this study to treat the place of God's Lamb in God's eternal pre-creation purpose.[2] Let me simply say here that God purposed to fulfill his eternal plan that governs all his ways and works in heaven and on earth in and by the person and work of Jesus Christ who is God's Alpha and Omega, the beginning, the center, and the end of all his will, his ways, and his works. Paul states in Ephesians 1:9: 'The mystery of [God's] will, according to his good pleasure,' he purposed to put into effect in Christ. And as we just saw in Ephesians 3:11 God 'accomplished' or 'effected' his eternal purpose 'in the Christ, Jesus our Lord'. When we restrict our comments then, as we will do here, to the biblical depictions concerning the Lamb of God given *after* the creation of the world we will gain from that disclosure an appreciation of the central place that the suffering Messiah as God's Lamb occupies in God's eternal purpose and in earth history.

The Old Testament uses at least eighteen nouns to designate the animals used in sacrifice,[3] all to be viewed as types of Jesus Christ as the antitypical Lamb of God.[4] The New Testament employs at least five nouns for the same purpose. Jesus himself stated in John 5:39: 'The [Old Testament] Scriptures … testify about me.' He also declared in John 5:46: 'Moses wrote about me.' And he declared in Luke 22:37: 'It is written [in Isa. 53:12]: "And he was numbered with the transgressors"; and I tell you that this must be fulfilled

---

[2] See my *A New Systematic Theology of the Christian Faith* (Second edition; Nashville, Tenn.: Thomas Nelson, 2002), 463-65 for fuller detail about the place of Christ in God's eternal purpose.

[3] *tāleh*, 'suckling lamb'; *kebhes*, 'lamb'; *kabhsāh*, 'ewe lamb'; *kar*, 'young ram'; *kesebh*, 'young ram'; *kisbhah*, 'young lamb'; *tsōn*, 'sheep'; *seh*, 'young lamb or kid'; *imm^erîm*, 'lambs'; *par*, 'bull, bullock'; *shōr*, 'bull, ox'; *tōr*, Aramaic for 'bull, ox'; *ēgel*, 'bull calf'; *ēz*, 'goat'; *attûdh*, 'ram, he-goat'; *sa'îr*, 'hairy goat'; *ayil*, 'ram'; and *d^ecar*, ram."

[4] *amnos*, 'lamb'; *arnion*, 'lamb'; *moskos*, 'calf'; *taurus*, 'bull'; and *tragos*, 'goat'.

in me. Yes, what is written about me is reaching its fulfillment' (see also Matt. 26:24, 31, 54, 56; Luke 18:31; Acts 8:32-35). After his resurrection he declared to Cleopas and his companion on the road to Emmaus: 'Did not the Messiah have to suffer these things [crucifixion and suffering] and then enter his glory [by his resurrection]?' Then Luke affirmed: 'And beginning with Moses and all the Prophets, he explained to them what was said in all the [Old Testament] Scriptures concerning himself' (Luke 24:26-27; see also John 13:18; 19:24, 28, 36-37; 20:9).[5] Later that evening to the disciples who had gathered together with others with them, Jesus stated: 'This is what I told you while I was still with you. Everything must be fulfilled that is written about me in the Law of Moses, the Prophets and the Psalms' (Luke 24:44). And what is this 'everything' about Jesus that is to be found throughout the Old Testament? It is, Jesus says, that 'the Messiah will suffer and rise from the dead' (Luke 24:46).

Peter also declared that 'all the prophets from Samuel on, as many as have spoken, have foretold these [New Testament] days' (Acts 3:22-24). And in 1 Peter 1:10-12 he affirmed that 'the Spirit of Christ [in the Old Testament prophets] predicted the sufferings of Christ and the glory that would follow'. And Paul declared that throughout his long missionary ministry of some thirty years he had never said anything 'beyond what the prophets and Moses said would happen – that the Messiah would suffer and, as the first to rise from the dead, would proclaim light to his own people and to the Gentiles' (Acts 26:22-23). So it is apparent from all these statements that Christ's Lamb work is to be found throughout the Old as well as the New Testament.

In this monograph we propose to examine the main vignettes that the Bible provides concerning the suffering Messiah as he is portrayed throughout Scripture as 'the Lamb of God [ho amnos tou theou] who bears away [airōn] the sin of the world' – the expression John the Baptist used (John 1:29, 36) to identify Jesus Christ as the New Testament's antitypical fulfillment of the Old Testament's typical sacrificial system.[6]

---

[5] Christians have often expressed the wish that they could have heard Jesus' interpretation of the Old Testament on that occasion. They can be assured, however, that both the apostles' sermons recorded in Acts and their apostolic letters reflect the major features of Christ's Emmaus road exposition by the way in which they interpret the Old Testament christologically.

[6] In the Old Testament, particularly in Exodus, Leviticus, and Numbers, eighty-five out of the total of ninety-six passages that refer to a lamb speak of the lamb as a sacrifice.

CHAPTER TWO

THE LAMB PROPHESIED:
GENESIS 3:15, 21

Biblical Messianism begins early in the Old Testament, highlighting the fact that it would include a tragic dimension within it. Immediately after Adam's tragic transgression of the 'covenant of works' that had been sovereignly imposed upon him by his Creator (Gen. 3:1-7; see Hos. 6:7) and that required of Adam that he personally and perfectly obey God's law for him, God came to his garden in Eden and in the hearing of the fallen Adam said to the serpent, the instrument of Satan, and by extension to Satan himself:

> I will put enmity between you and the woman, and between your offspring and hers; he will crush your head, and you will strike his heel (Gen. 3:15; see Rom. 16:20).

Long have Christian theologians recognized in God's 'declaration of war' against Satan and his kingdom of evil both the inauguration of the 'covenant of grace' and God's first gracious declaration to fallen mankind of the prospect of salvation from sin. Not without good reason has this divine promise been designated the 'first gospel proclamation' (*protevangelium*). This prophetic promise is given in 'seed-form', true enough, but God clearly predicted that *someone* out of the human race, namely, 'the woman's Seed,' although fatally 'wounded' in the conflict,[1] would destroy the Serpent and his reign of evil. 'It is surely significant,' John Murray observes, '...that the first promise of

---

[1] Nothing is said here about the 'deeper magic', to borrow C. S. Lewis's phrase from his *The Lion, the Witch and the Wardrobe* (New York: Macmillan, 1950), 132, concerning the Seed's resurrection from death. That truth is made known symbolically in Genesis 22:5 (see Heb. 11:17-19).

11

redemptive grace, the first beam of redemptive light that fell upon our fallen first parents, was in terms of the destruction of the tempter.'[2] In this same connection he writes elsewhere:

> It is most significant that the work of Christ, which is so central in our Christian faith, is essentially a work of destruction that terminates upon the power and work of Satan. This is not a peripheral or incidental feature of redemption. It is an integral aspect of its accomplishment.[3]

God's prophetic declaration of Satan's destruction, here foretold, (1) found the *ground* of its fulfillment in the Temptation, in which Christ 'bound the strong man', thereby 'overpowering him and taking away his armor' (Mark 1:12-13; Matt. 4:1-11, see 12:28-29; Luke 4:1-13, see 11:21-22) and in his 'Lamb work' at Calvary, thereby 'disarming [Satan's] powers and authorities, making a public spectacle of them and triumphing over them by the cross' (John 12:31b; Col. 2:13c-15; Heb. 2:14-15); (2) is finding the *continuation* of this fulfillment in Christ's current reign at his Father's right hand during which he is putting all of his enemies under his feet (1 Cor. 15:24-25); and (3) will find the *consummation* of this fulfillment when Christ as the glorified Lamb in the Day of his wrath (Rev. 6:16) returns as the Judge of all the earth to conquer completely both his and our enemies (Rev. 17:14; 19:11–20:10) – not three different fulfillments but three aspects of one complex fulfillment.

Here, I would suggest, is the first and the grandest occurrence in Scripture of what biblical interpreters term the literary device of *inclusio* (inclusion), that is, 'a kind of literary envelope that subtly clasps in its embrace'[4] an overarching theme by placing at the beginning and end of a given literary piece like bookends similar literary features that then govern everything that the author inserts between these ideas. At the beginning of mankind's lapsarian history, immediately after Adam's fall, God prophesied concerning Christ's destructive work that he would conduct against Satan and his kingdom; at the end of this lapsarian age according to John's Revelation,

---

[2]John Murray, *Redemption – Accomplished and Applied* (Grand Rapids: Eerdmans, 1955), 49.

[3]John Murray, 'The Fall of Man,' in *Collected Writings of John Murray* (Edinburgh: Banner of Truth, 1977), 2:67-68. We will say more about this destructive work of the Lamb in Chapters 11 and 12.

[4]D. A. Carson, *The Gospel According to John* (Grand Rapids: Eerdmans, 1991), 135.

Christus Victor will consummate his destructive work against Satan and his kingdom. Everything in the Bible between these events supports and brings this theme to expression. Latent then in everything the Bible affirms about Christ's '*Lamb* work' is the motif of his conquering, destructive work conducted against Satan and his demonic forces![5]

While I concur with Geerhardus Vos who observes quite correctly: '... it is unhistorical to carry back into the O.T. mind our *developed* doctrinal consciousness of these matters,'[6] it is also possible to address the meaning of Old Testament texts and the Old Testament saints' understanding of redemption so one-sidedly from the 'biblical-theological' perspective that one permits the hermeneutic of that discipline to overpower the 'analogy of Scripture' principle of systematic theology,[7] and as a result neither the teaching of the Old Testament itself nor what the New Testament writers

---

[5]Should the reader like to see other examples of *inclusio*, three may be seen in John's Gospel, the first one geographical, the last two theological. Scholars have often observed that 2:1–4:54 moves from Cana to Cana, enabling us better to see the geographical boundaries and movement of the text.

Theologically, how does John begin his Gospel? By declaring that the Word 'was God' (John 1:1). How does he conclude his Gospel prologue in John 1:18? By declaring that Jesus Christ, the unique [Son, himself] God, who is in the bosom of the Father, has 'exegeted' him. Thus the boundaries of John's prologue are clearly marked. How does John conclude his entire Gospel? By recording Thomas's ringing declaration concerning Jesus: '[You are] my Lord and my God' (John 20:28)! Thus John brings his Gospel to its climax by presenting Jesus Christ as the risen Lord, victorious over sin, sorrow, doubt, and death. This suggests that John intended *everything* in his Gospel to serve as supporting evidence for his declared purpose in writing his Gospel, namely, to demonstrate that Jesus Christ as the Messiah is both the Son of God and God himself and that he should be trusted (see John 20:30-31).

[6]Geerhardus Vos, *Biblical Theology* (Grand Rapids: Eerdmans, 1948), 164, emphasis supplied.

[7]An example of this 'one-sidedness' may be found in Walter C. Kaiser, Jr.'s *Toward an Exegetical Theology: Biblical Exegesis for Preaching and Teaching* (Grand Rapids: Baker, 1981) in which he insists in many places (for example, 82, 134-40) upon what he calls 'the analogy of (antecedent) Scripture'. What he means by this phrase is this: in determining the author's intended meaning in a given passage, in no case is the exegete, in order to 'unpack the meaning or to enhance the usability of the individual text which is the object of [his] study' (140), to use teaching from a passage written or spoken later than the biblical statement being analyzed. In arriving at the author's intended meaning, the exegete must restrict himself to a study of the passage itself and to 'affirmations found in passages that have *preceded* in time the passage under study' (136, emphasis original). Kaiser's canon grows out of his concern to give the discipline of biblical theology its

expressly report or imply that the Old Testament meant and that the Old Testament saints knew about the suffering Messiah and his resurrection from the dead is given its rightful due.

In my opinion Vos himself commits this error when he construes 'the seed of the woman' in Genesis 3:15 in a collective rather than a personal sense:

> As to the word 'seed' there is no reason to depart from the collective sense in either case. The seed of the serpent *must* be collective, and this determines the sense of the seed of the woman.[8]

But it does not necessarily follow because the seed of the serpent is collective that the seed of the woman must also be collective. I would submit that it was precisely of Jesus Christ that God spoke here just as Paul insisted that it was

---

just due with its vision of the progressiveness of revelation (137). To permit subsequent revelation to determine a given author's intention is to 'level off' the process of revelation in a way overly favorable to the interests of systematic theology. See my critique of Kaiser's canon in *Contending for the Faith: Lines in the Sand that Strengthen the Church* (Ross-shire, Scotland: Mentor, 2005), 363-66.

[8] Vos, *Biblical Theology*, 54. After Vos urges that it is the collective sense that must be placed on the 'seed of the woman', he acknowledges: '… indirectly, the possibility is *hinted at* that in striking this fatal blow the seed of the woman will be concentrated in one person, for it should be noticed that it is not the seed of the serpent but the serpent itself whose head will be bruised. In the former half of the curse the two seeds are contrasted; here the woman's seed and the serpent. This suggests that as at the climax of the struggle the serpent's seed will be represented by the serpent, in the same manner [that is, at the climax of the struggle] the woman's seed *may find representation* in a single person' (54-5, emphasis supplied).

But having said this, Vos then backpedals and declares: '…we are not warranted, however, in seeking an exclusively personal reference to the Messiah here, as though He alone were meant by "the woman's seed." O.T. Revelation approaches the concept of a personal Messiah very gradually' (55).

Meredith G. Kline, 'Genesis,' in *The New Bible Commentary: Revised* (London: Inter-Varsity, 1970), 85, seems to concur with Vos's basic position: '*Between your seed and her seed*. Beyond the woman, the whole family of the true humanity, becoming her spiritual seed by faith, will stand in continuing conflict with those descendants of fallen Adam who obdurately manifest spiritual sonship to the devil…. *He shall bruise your head, and you shall bruise his heel*. The "you" still contending in the remote future points past the mere serpent to Satan. This focusing on an individual from one side in connection with the eventual encounter suggests that the *he* too is not the woman's seed collectively but their individual champion.'

precisely of Jesus Christ that God later spoke in his reference to Abraham's 'Seed' in Genesis 13:15 and 17:8 (Gal. 3:16). Furthermore, it is inexplicable why Vos makes nothing of the 'death wound' that 'the woman's Seed' would experience in his conflict with the *Serpent*, *not* the Serpent's seed, stating only that the *protevangelium* promised that '*somehow* out of the human race a fatal blow will come which shall crush the head of the serpent'.[9] I would not say 'somehow' here. I would contend, on the basis of the clear allusion to his death in the *protevangelium*, that from the very beginning of redemptive history the saints' everlasting hope rested in the triumphant 'conflict work' carried out by a specific individual, namely, the *mortally wounded* 'Seed of the woman'. The Seed's 'conflict work' is primally depicted a few verses later in Genesis 3:21 when Yahweh God took the skin of a *single* animal and made garments for the naked pair who were experiencing the shame of physical nakedness that is only the *external* reflex of the *internal* nakedness of the sin-burdened mind before God. This divine activity points up the truth that Adam and Eve were not wrong in seeking a 'covering' (Gen. 3:7). Where they went wrong was in seeking a covering in *their* works rather than seeking God's forgiveness that is grounded in the Seed's 'conflict work' depicted by the animal skin. For that is precisely what the skin depicted: a *sacrifice* for sin, becoming thereby the *first* tangible depiction in history of the Lamb slain from the creation of the world. Keil and Delitzsch write:

> By selecting the skins of beasts for the clothing of the first men, and therefore causing the death or slaughter of beasts for that purpose, [God] showed them how they might ... sacrifice animal life for the preservation of human; so that this act of God laid the foundation for the [biblical] sacrifices.[10]

But if the 'he' may be (Vos) or is to be (Kline) construed, not collectively, but as an individual, why is 'the woman's seed' not an individual as well, since 'the woman's seed' is the antecedent of the 'he'? Are we to believe, *contra Westminster Confession of Faith* I/ix, that 'seed' here has or may have a dual meaning?

[9] Vos, *Biblical Theology*, 54, emphasis supplied.

[10] C. F. Keil and F. Delitzsch, *Biblical Commentary on the Old Testament: The Pentateuch*, translated by James Martin (Reprint; Grand Rapids: Eerdmans, n.d.), I, 106. Meredith G. Kline concurs, writing in 'Genesis,' in *The New Bible Commentary Revised*, edited by D. Guthrie and J. A. Motyer (Grand Rapids: Eerdmans, 1970), 85: 'This remedy [clothing Adam and Eve] for the obstacle to their approach to God (*see* 3:10) symbolized God's purpose to restore men to fellowship with him. The sinner's shame, as a religious problem, could not be covered by their own efforts (see 3:7). Implied in God's provision is an act

Thus begins the history of Old Testament Messianism and more specifically the doctrine of God's Lamb slain for the sins of his elect, both of which run right through biblical revelation. If one will get right the principles of redemptive theology that are set forth in Genesis 3 it will help him to stay away from doctrinal error as he moves through the rest of Scripture.

---

of animal sacrifice; what is explicit, however, is not the sacrificial mode but remedial result.' Regrettably, Vos, *Biblical Theology*, 173, does not see the divine institution of expiatory sacrifice in Genesis 3:21 because 'the word used for this act of God is not the technical term used in the law for the covering of sin by sacrifice'. This is hardly a sound reason for rejecting the obvious.

CHAPTER THREE

THE LAMB SYMBOLIZED:
GENESIS 22:1-14

With God's election of and command to Abraham to leave his country, his kindred, and his father's house, the covenant of grace, inaugurated in Genesis 3:15, assumed a covenantal form in and by the Abrahamic Covenant that became definitive for all time to come. All recorded biblical history prior to Genesis 12 stands as introduction to God's covenant with Abraham while all that follows the Abrahamic Covenant is the outworking of God's promises covenantally given to him and to his seed. By a confident faith generated by God's gracious quickening, Abraham believed and obeyed God

and went, even though he did not know where he was going. By faith he made his home in the promised land like a stranger in a foreign country; he lived in tents, as did Isaac and Jacob, who were heirs with him of the same promise. For he was looking forward to the city with foundations, whose architect and builder is God (Heb. 11:8-10).

And so by God's grace Abraham became the spiritual father of all who believe (Gal. 3:7-9) and heir of the world (Rom. 4:13). God's promise that in Abraham *all* the families of the earth would be blessed indicates that his election should be viewed as a *particularistic* means to a glorious *universalistic* end – the salvation of an elect seed out of every kindred, nation, and tongue. But all this appeared to be placed in jeopardy when God commanded Abraham: 'Take your son, your only son, Isaac, whom you love, [the son according to Gen. 17:19-21 and 21:12 through whom Abraham's seed was covenantally to continue], and go to the land of Moriah. Sacrifice him there as a burnt offering on one of the mountains I will tell you about' (Gen. 22:2). As we shall see, there are a number of intriguing symbolic events and statements[1] in this oft-expounded incident,[2] the first being that God specified that Isaac

---

[1]In his *Biblical Theology*, 161-62 (emphasis supplied), Geerhardus Vos offers some very valuable insights on biblical symbols and biblical types:

'A symbol is in its religious significance something that profoundly portrays a certain fact or principle or relationship of a spiritual nature in a visible form. The things it pictures are of present existence and present application. They are in force at the time in which the symbol operates. With the same thing, regarded as a type, it is different. A typical thing is prospective; it relates to what will become real or applicable in the future....

'The main problem to understand is, how the same system of portrayals can have served at one and the same time in a symbolical and a typical capacity. Obviously this would have been impossible if the things portrayed had been in each case different or diverse, unrelated to each other. If something is an accurate picture of a certain reality, then it would seem disqualified by this very fact for pointing to another future reality of a quite different nature. The solution of the problem lies in this, that the things symbolized and the things typified are not different sets of things. They are in reality the same things, only different in this respect that they come first on a lower stage of development in redemption, and then again, in a later period, on a higher stage. Thus what is symbolical with regard to the already existing edition of the fact or truth becomes typical, prophetic, of the later, final edition [the antitype] of that same fact or truth. From this it will be perceived that *a type can never be a type independently of its being first a symbol. The gateway to the house of typology is at the farther end of the house of symbolism.* This is the fundamental rule to be observed in ascertaining what elements in the O.T. are typical, and wherein the things corresponding to them as antitypes consist. Only after having discovered what a thing symbolizes, can we legitimately proceed to put the question what it typifies, for the latter can never be aught else than the former lifted to a higher plane.'

If one heeds Vos's insights one will be spared making absurd and extravagant claims for things as 'types' that really are not types at all because they either fail to symbolize things of religious significance that profoundly portray certain facts in their original existence and application or are said to point to future realities that are of a quite different nature, claims that 'have produced in better-trained minds a distaste for typology.'

[2]The theologically liberal portion of the church has expounded this entire event as an aetiological legend standing in opposition to all human sacrifice. Vos, *Biblical Theology*, 106-7, however, is right when he counsels:

'It is well to be cautious in committing oneself to that critical opinion, for it strikes at the very heart of the atonement. The rejection of the 'blood theology' as

was to be sacrificed on a mountain in the land of Moriah (perhaps named proleptically from this event),[3] which fact in itself, since later 'Solomon … built the temple of the Lord in Jerusalem on Mount Moriah' on the property that, according to God's instructions, David purchased from Ornan the Jebusite for an altar site (2 Sam. 24:18-19, 24-25; 2 Chron. 3:1), 'links this sacrifice through its locality with the [typical] sacrificial cultus in the temple at Jerusalem'[4] and thereby to Christ as *the* antitypical Lamb of God.

At God's behest Abraham and Isaac with two servants immediately set out from Beersheba for the sacrificial site, and 'on the third day Abraham … saw the place in the distance' (Gen. 22:4), which fact suggests that Isaac, as far as Abraham was concerned, had been, symbolically speaking, 'as good as dead' for those three days of travel. When they reached the site of sacrifice Abraham placed the wood he had brought along for the burnt offering on Isaac,[5] and he carried the fire and the knife. Isaac then asked his father: 'The fire and the wood are here, but where is the lamb [*seh*] for the burnt offering?' Abraham prophetically declared: 'God will see [our need and provide] [*yir'eh*; the imperfect form of *rā'āh*, implying the future] for himself the lamb [*seh*] for the burnt offering, my son' (Gen. 20:8). When Abraham declared that God would see their need and, by implication, provide the lamb for the

---

a remnant of a very barbaric type of primitive religion rests on such a basis … by the interposition of the Angel and the pointing out of the ram in the thicket [what this aspect of the passage teaches is] that the substitution of one life for another life would be acceptable to God. Not sacrifice of human life as such, but the sacrifice of average sinful human life is deprecated by the O. T.'

Said another way, the God of Scripture is not opposed *in principle* to animal sacrifices or, for that matter, to all *human* sacrifice but only to *sinful* human sacrifice because such sacrifices accomplish nothing before him. To see this, one has only to recall that it was God himself who 'did not spare his own Son but gave him up for us all' (Rom. 8:32) and who willed to 'crush him and cause him to suffer' (Isa. 53:10). Indeed, it is only because of the sinless human sacrifice that the Son of God himself became – that alone prevails before God – that anyone will ever be forgiven and go to heaven when he dies.

[3] The name 'Moriah' (*môrîyyāh*), from the root *rā'āh*, meaning 'to see [a need and hence to provide],' with the prefixed locative *m*, designating a 'place' and the suffixed *yah*, meaning 'Yahweh', literally means something on the order of 'the place where Yahweh saw [and provided a sacrifice].'

[4] Vos, *Biblical Theology*, 108.

[5] Many early Christian writers saw Isaac's carrying the wood as a type of Christ carrying his cross.

burnt offering, he either believed, if God intended that he should actually carry out the divine command, that God would raise Isaac from the dead since God had promised him that his future seed would come through Isaac's line (Heb. 11:17-19),[6] or he believed that God would provide a substitute sacrifice to take Isaac's place (which is in fact what took place), prophesying as the prophet that he was (Gen. 20:7) – doubtless more fully than even he realized – also concerning the antitypical Lamb of God who would take away the world's sin. In either of these cases Isaac, as the human sacrificial lamb and attached as his 'lamb role' was in this episode to Abraham's prophetic declaration, both symbolized and typically depicted the antitypical Lamb of God, and his being spared symbolized his resurrection from the dead after three days (see Heb. 11:17-19).

In God's halting the sacrifice of Isaac and providing as his substitute the 'thorn-crowned' male sheep (*'ayil*; LXX: *krios*) caught by his horns in a

---

[6]The reader should not overlook the fact that Abraham had specifically informed the two servants in Genesis 22:5: 'We [the lad and I] will worship and then *we will come back* [*nāshûbhāh*, a cohortative *plural* form showing confidence or determination] to you.' So clearly Abraham believed, were Isaac actually to die, that God would raise him from the dead. When Isaac was not sacrificed, Abraham, 'symbolically speaking [*en parabolç*; literally, 'in a symbol'],' received Isaac back from death (Heb. 11:19) after three days.

Scholars have long pondered what specific Old Testament text Paul had in mind when he wrote that Christ 'was raised on the third day *according to the Scriptures*' (1 Cor. 15:4). There are not many Old Testament texts from which to choose. Most frequently Hosea 6:2 ('After two days he will revive us; on the third day he will restore us, that we may live in his presence') and sometimes Jonah 1:17 (on the basis of Matthew 12:30) and 2 Kings 20:5 ('On the third day you shall go up to the house of the Lord') are proffered. The problem with Hosea 6:2, considered the one most promising by many scholars, is that it speaks of *our* resurrection if it speaks of resurrection at all. The problem with Jonah 1:17 is that it requires the Matthean verse to make the connection. And the problem with 2 Kings 20:5 is that the passage does not speak of resurrection as such at all but rather of Hezekiah's trip to the temple on the third day *after* his healing from a terminal illness.

I would suggest, however, that the Moriah event in Genesis 22, rarely if ever considered as a possibility, is quite likely the best choice when all things are considered. Abraham's statement in Genesis 22:5 clearly intimates that Isaac would be resurrected on the third day after God's command to sacrifice him during which period Abraham had viewed Isaac as dead, and the Author of Hebrews expressly states that Abraham 'symbolically speaking' received Isaac back from death at that time. One has only to comprehend Isaac's *symbolic* death and resurrection as a type of Christ's *actual* death and resurrection to comprehend how Paul could write that Christ 'was raised on the third day according to the Scriptures.'

thicket of thorns we see vividly depicted the typical fulfillment of Abraham's prophetic declaration that God would provide the antitypical sacrifice, this fulfillment, of course, *via* the equally typical protocols of the later Levitical legislation, being in the person of Jesus, the Lamb of God. Accordingly, Abraham called that place *Yhwh yir'eh* ('the Lord will see [our need and provide (the lamb)]'), hence the name 'Moriah' – 'the place where Yahweh saw [our need and provided (the lamb)].' And Moses informs us that as a result a saying was born that day that carried such significance that some six hundred years later in his day it was still being cited: 'On the mountain of Yahweh he will appear [the *niph'al* form of *rā'āh*] [and provide (the lamb)]' (Gen. 22:14), very likely a prophetic allusion, whether always consciously intended as such, to the antitypical Lamb's offering up of himself to God in sacrifice on Mount Zion. Keil and Delitzsch write in this regard:

> …the event acquires prophetic importance for the Church of the Lord, to which the place of sacrifice points with peculiar clearness, viz. Mount Moriah, upon which under the legal economy all the typical sacrifices were offered to Jehovah; upon which, in the fulness of time, God the Father gave up His only-begotten Son as an atoning sacrifice for the sins of the whole world, that by this one true sacrifice the shadows of the typical sacrifices might be rendered both real and true. If therefore the appointment of Moriah as the scene of the sacrifice of Isaac, and the offering of a ram in his stead, were primarily only typical in relation to the significance and intent of the Old Testament institution of sacrifice; this type already pointed to the antitype to appear in the future, when the eternal love of the heavenly Father would perform what it had demanded of Abraham; that is to say, when God would not spare His only Son, but give Him up to the real death, which Isaac suffered only in spirit, that we also might die with Christ spiritually, and rise with Him to everlasting life (Rom. viii. 32, vi. 5, etc.).[7]

Because of God's covenant fidelity Christians today can now say: 'On the mountain of Yahweh he *has* appeared [and *has* provided the required Lamb].'

Should someone ask, if all this is so, why the New Testament does not do more than it does with this bit of Genesis material,[0] I would say, first, that the New Testament writers used Old Testament material only when the

---

[7]Keil and Delitzsch, *Biblical Commentary on the Old Testament: The Pentateuch*, I, 253.

[8]It should be noted that in two New Testament passages this story is expressly mentioned – James 2:21-22 employing it to provide probative evidence that Abraham's

latter lent itself to their specific *ad hoc* topics; if those topics did not call for the support of Old Testament material such as this they did not use it. I would say, second, with Vos that 'the mere fact that no writer in the N. T. refers to a certain trait as typical, affords no proof of its lacking typical significance....'[9] Of course, it is inevitable that into this kind of interpretation of O. T. figures an element of uncertainty must enter. But after all this is an element that enters into all [extra-biblical] exegesis.'[10]

---

faith which was the instrument of his justification was a living and vital faith, Hebrews 11:17-19 employing it to highlight Abraham's vital faith in God's promise that his offspring would come through Isaac even if it meant that God would raise Isaac from death – and its influence may well be traced both in Romans 8:32, which seems to echo the LXX Greek of Genesis 22:16, and in John 8:56, which may well provide the reason that Abraham 'rejoiced at the thought of seeing [Christ's] day; he saw it [in God's provision of the ram in the stead of Isaac] and was glad.'

[9]Bishop Herbert Marsh's dictum in his *Lectures on the Criticism and Interpretation of the Bible* (London, 1838), 373, that the interpreter should regard as Old Testament types only what the New Testament expressly declares to be so seems to me to be extreme and without scriptural warrant.

[10]Vos, *Biblical Theology*, 162-63.

CHAPTER FOUR

THE LAMB TYPIFIED:
EXODUS 12:1-13

The patriarchal period came to an end with Jacob's family moving to Egypt because of a severe famine in Palestine. There Jacob's son Joseph, who in God's marvelous providence had risen to political prominence in Egypt, protected them, and Jacob's family prospered. But with the passage of time a Pharaoh came to power 'who did not know Joseph' (Exod. 1:8) and who enslaved Jacob's descendants. In due course God raised up Moses as Israel's deliverer from Egyptian bondage, this great exodus redemption being recorded in Exodus 2–12.

As *the* Old Testament redemptive event *par excellence* the night of the paschal deliverance[1] was to mark the beginning of the year in Israel and all future events were to be dated from this historical event (Exod. 12:2). This redemptive deliverance was grounded in and sprang from God's sovereign, loving, elective purpose and was accomplished by God's almighty power. But in spite of these two facts the exodus event actually delivered only those who

---

[1]That it is not reading too much into the event of the exodus to characterize it as a *redemptive* event is borne out by the fact that the biblical text represents it precisely this way:

Exodus 6:6: 'I will free you from being slaves to them, and *I will redeem you* with an outstretched arm and with mighty acts of judgment.'

Exodus 15:13: 'In your unfailing love you will lead the people *you have redeemed*.'

Deuteronomy 8:7: '...it was because the Lord loved you ... that he brought you out with a mighty hand and *redeemed you* from the land of slavery.'

Deuteronomy 9:26: 'O Sovereign Lord, do not destroy your people, your own inheritance, that *you redeemed* by your great power and brought out of Egypt with a mighty hand.'

availed themselves of the expiation of sin afforded by the efficacious covering of the blood of the Lord's 'paschal lamb' (*pesach*, Exod. 12:11-13, 21-23, 24-27).[2] Vos writes: 'Grace could not, notwithstanding its sovereignty, be exercised without an accompanying atonement.'[3] Thus the Lord declared: 'The blood [of the paschal lamb] will be a sign for you on the houses where you are; and when I see the blood I will pass over you [*ûphasachtî ʰlēkem*]' (Exod. 12:13; see also 12:23).

That the paschal lamb is to be regarded as a 'sacrifice' is expressly declared in Exodus 12:27 (*zebhach pesach*, '[the] sacrifice of [the] paschal lamb') and 34:25 (*zebhach hag happāsach*, 'the sacrifice of the feast of the paschal lamb'). Its efficacy is to be attached not to its identification of the Israelite dwellings that were to be spared but to its *sacrificial* character.[4] As a biblical principle, wherever the blood of a *sacrifice* is shed as God prescribes so that he stays his judgment against the sinner one may infer that expiation or the 'covering' of sin has been effected. Moreover, because the blood of the paschal lamb was to be applied to the home by a sprig of hyssop that figures everywhere as an instrument of purification, one may assume that purification from sin is also present in the paschal celebration. The notion of purification is also brought out in Exodus 12:15-20 which teaches that the paschal celebration initiated the Feast of Unleavened Bread, a week-long observance during which all leaven was to be removed from the Israelite's house and only unleavened bread was to be eaten.[5] Thus the exodus event came to its climax precisely in terms of the divinely required substitutionary atonement provided by the paschal lamb under whose 'covering' each *purified* Israelite household had to place its confidence if it was to be spared the death of its firstborn.

---

[2]The noun *pesach* is from the Hebrew root *pāsach* that literally means 'to leap, to hop', then 'to jump over', then 'to pass over' or 'to spare', as here in Exodus 12:13, 23.

[3]Vos, *Biblical Theology*, 134-35.

[4]Vos, *Biblical Theology*, 135.

[5]Paul employs the close connection in the Old Testament between the Passover celebration and the observance of the Week of Unleavened Bread in his dealing with the case of immorality in the Corinthian church in 1 Corinthians 5. He writes: 'Get rid of the old yeast that you may be a new batch without yeast – as you really are. For Christ, our Passover lamb, has been sacrificed. Therefore let us keep the Festival [of Unleavened Bread], not with the old yeast, the yeast of malice and wickedness, but with bread without yeast, the bread of sincerity and truth' (1 Cor. 5:7-8). Paul's point is that since their antitypical Passover lamb, even Christ, has been sacrified, Christians should now be 'observing the Festival of Unleaven Bread' in the sense that they should put away from themselves all wickedness. Therefore, he instructed them, 'Expel the wicked man from among you' (1 Cor. 5:13).

That the paschal lamb had typical significance pointing toward Christ as the antitypical Lamb of God is expressly declared by Paul in 1 Corinthians 5:7: '…our paschal lamb [*to pāskā*], even Christ, has been sacrificed.' And because God specifically states in Exodus 12:9 that the paschal lamb was to be eaten neither raw [*nā*] nor boiled with water [*mᵉbhushshāl bammāyim*] but rather roasted with fire [*tselî 'ēsh*] I find intriguing the speculations (for that is admittedly what they are) that would seek to answer the questions: 'What specifically, antitypically, would a "raw Christ" be?' 'What specifically, antitypically, would a "boiled Christ" be?' 'What specifically, antitypically, would a "Christ roasted with fire" be?' Since any distinctions here cannot be in the fact of Christ's death as such because the Israelite family would have had to put the paschal lamb to death whether eaten raw, boiled, or roasted with fire, very likely, then, when these specific instructions are applied to Christ as the antitypical Lamb, they indicate a specific character of, and heart attitude toward, Christ's death. A 'raw Christ' would likely be the liberal's Christ whose bloody death is viewed simply as that of a martyr with no intrinsic saving benefits at all; the 'boiled Christ' is the Arminian's Christ whose death, while intended for all, is so weak and lacking in power to accomplish that for which it was intended, namely, the salvation of *all* men, that in itself it too intrinsically actually saves no one, and the 'Christ roasted with fire' is the biblical and Reformed Christ whose Lamb work on the cross entailed in a figure even his enduring the pains of hell fire for his people, thereby intrinsically saving them to the uttermost.[6]

---

[6]Keil and Delitzsch in their *Biblical Commentary on the Old Testament: The Pentateuch*, II, 14-15, offer another view: 'By boiling … the integrity of the animal would have been destroyed … through the fact that, in boiling, the substance of the flesh is more or less dissolved.' Citing Baehr they continue: 'By avoiding the breaking of the bones, the animal was preserved in complete integrity, undisturbed and entire. The sacrificial lamb to be eaten was to be thoroughly and perfectly whole, and at the time of eating was to appear as a perfect whole, and therefore as one; for it is not what is dissected, divided, broken in pieces, but only what is whole, that is *eo ipso* one. There was no other reason for this, than that all who took part in this one whole animal, i.e. all who ate of it, should look upon themselves as one whole, one community, like those who eat the New Testament Passover, the body of Christ (1 Cor. v. 7), of whom the apostle says (1 Cor. x. 17), "There is one bread, and so we, being many, are one body: for we are all partakers of one body." The preservation of Christ, so that not a bone was broken, had the same signification; and God ordained this that He might appear as the true paschal lamb, that was slain for the sins of the world.' The problem I have with their suggestion is that Keil and Delitzsch offer no meaning for the 'raw Christ' that is consistent with their 'boiled Christ,' something they must do if their suggestion about the 'boiled Christ' is to be adopted.

CHAPTER FIVE

THE LAMB SIGNIFIED:
EXODUS 25–40; LEVITICUS 8–9

In addition to the Ten Commandments – God's binding moral law for all mankind that he intended as an instrument to restrain the ungodly, to drive the sinner to Christ (Gal. 3:19), and to guide the Christian as the covenant norm for living – God gave to his redeemed people at Sinai instructions concerning both the building of the wilderness tabernacle and the institution of the Aaronic priesthood that would serve at the tabernacle (and later at the Solomonic temple), each in its own way signifying the Lamb work of Christ.

THE TABERNACLE: (EXOD. 25–28, 30, 35–40)
Imagine a fifteen-by-forty-five-foot portable prefabricated tent – 'an artist's delight – a riot of color, texture, and design'[1] – constructed of 29 talents and 730 shekels of gold (about 1 metric ton), 100 talents and 1,775 shekels of silver (3¾ metric tons), and 70 talents and 2,400 shekels of bronze (2½ tons) (Exod. 38:24-31), plus an assortment of fine wood, fine tapestries of a variety of colors, and animal hides. This was the tabernacle or 'tent of meeting' (this expression is found about 130 times) where God met with his people to declare his will to them (Exod. 33:9). It was Israel's house of worship in the wilderness built by redeemed slaves under the construction management of two men, Bezalel and Oholiab, during their first year at Sinai. In God's providence the project was financed by freewill offerings from the farewell gifts the Egyptians gave to the people of Israel when they

---

[1]'Tabernacle,' *Dictionary of Biblical Imagery*, edited by Leland Ryken, James C. Wilhoit, and Tremper Longman III (Downers Grove, Ill.: InterVarsity, 1998), 837.

left Egypt. We have no way of knowing the monetary value of the building material for such a structure,[2] but if it were being constructed today at mid-December 2005 world market prices, it could not be built for less than well over 19,703,200 USA dollars,[3] that works out to be well over $29,190 per square foot! Never before or since has such a costly pre-fab been built, the epitome of simplicity to assemble and to dismantle by the eight and a half thousand custodians composed of the three Levite families, the Kohathites, the Gershonites, and the Merarites[4] who were responsible for the duty of dismantling and transporting the tabernacle when the sheltering cloud of God's presence moved and erecting the tabernacle when the cloud stopped moving. When it was erected it was to stand in the center of the camp with the tribes of Issachar, Judah, and Zebulun camping on the east, the tribes of Asher, Dan, and Naphtali camping on the north, the tribes of Benjamin, Ephraim, and Manasseh camping on the west, and the tribes of Gad, Reuben, and Simeon camping on the south.

While God expended only two chapters recounting the creation of the world he expended *thirteen* chapters in Exodus to the assembling of and the priestly service to be conducted at the tabernacle (Exod. 25–31, 35–40). The tabernacle was to be built 'according to the pattern that was shown to Moses in the mount' (Exod. 25:9, 40; 26:30; Acts 7:44) because, according to the Author of Hebrews, it was to be an exact copy and shadow of the true tabernacle into which Christ entered with his own blood as the redeemed saint's High Priest after the order of Melchizedek (Heb. 8:2, 5; 9:21-28).[5] The detailed instructions for the construction of the tabernacle, the

---

[2]The articles 'Gold' and 'Silver' in *Dictionary of Biblical Imagery* both note, however, that gold and silver were regarded in Old Testament times as precious metals of superior value.

[3]This figure is reached by adding the current value of approximately 1 metric ton (2200 pounds) of gold at $526 per ounce ($18,515,200), 3¾ metric tons of silver at $9 per ounce ($1,188,000), plus the unestablished values of the 2½ metric tons of bronze, plus jewels, fine woods, and fine tapestries.

[4]Robert Murray McCheyne composed a delightful poem of six line about these three families:

The Kohathites upon their shoulders bear
the holy vessels covered all with care.
The Gershonites receive an easier charge,
two wagons full of cords and curtains large.
Merari's sons four ponderous waggons load
with boards and pillars of the House of God.

prototype of the Solomonic temple, are found in Exodus 25–30, including detailed instructions concerning the building of

- the ark of the covenant (25:10-22),
- the table of the bread of the Presence (25:23-30),
- the lampstand (25:31-40),
- the linen curtains (26:1-6),
- the coverings (26:7-14),
- the boards and tenons (26:15-25),
- the crossbars (26:26-30),
- the veil (26:31-35),
- the entrance screen (26:36-37),
- the bronze altar (27:1-8),
- the courtyard (27:9-19),
- the altar of incense (30:1-6), and
- the wash basin (30:17-21).

Gleason L. Archer, Jr. describes the appearance of the completed tabernacle in this manner:

(1) The outer hangings of the court enclosed a perimeter measuring fifty by one hundred cubits.... (2) The tabernacle itself was a large tent measuring ten by thirty cubits (the cubit being a little over a foot and a half) and curtained off into two sections, the holy place and the holy of holies [or most holy place]. (3) In the court outside of the tabernacle and situated in front of its curtain door or 'outer veil' was placed the 'great' altar or altar of burnt offering covered with bronze, on which all the offerings were presented, both the blood sacrifices and the grain offerings.... (4) Between the brazen altar and the entrance curtain [of the tabernacle] stood the laver, a large basin made of bronze, in which priests had to wash their hands and their feet before entering the holy place.... The tabernacle itself consisted of two compartments. (5) The holy place, measuring twenty by ten cubits, contained three sacred objects. (6) On the north or right side, was the ... table and bread of the Presence on which were laid out twelve fresh loaves of fine flour every Sabbath. It undoubtedly typified Christ as the bread of life, and symbolized Israel also (the twelve tribes) as the people of God

---

[5] I will say more on pages 35 and 36 about the meaning of the true Tabernacle into which Christ entered with his own blood.

presented before him as a living sacrifice. (7) On the south or left side, stood the lampstand or 'candlestick' with its seven oil lamps, typifying Christ as the light of the world, who by his Spirit performs the perfect work of God (symbolized by the number seven), enabling His people to shine forth a light of testimony to the world (cf. Zech. 4). (8) On the west was located the small golden altar, the altar of incense, used only for the offering of incense in front of the inner curtain which separated the holy place from the holy of holies. This golden altar probably typified the effectual prayer of Christ the Intercessor.... (9) The inner curtain typified the veil of Christ's flesh (cf. Heb. 10:20) which had to be rent (as it was at the hour Christ died, Matt. 27:15) if the barrier was to be removed which separated God from his people. (10) Within the holy of holies, measuring ten by ten cubits, there was only (11) the ark of the covenant, consisting of a chest 2.5 by 1.5 cubits, covered by a lid of solid gold wrought into the shape of two cherubim facing each other with outstretched wings and looking downward at the surface of the lid. (12) This lid was called the 'propitiatory'..., rendered by the KJV as 'mercy seat,' and upon it the high priest sprinkled the blood of the sin offering on the Day of Atonement, thus typifying Christ's atonement (Heb. 9:12) in the very presence of God. The ark thus represented the presence of God in the midst of his people; it was his footstool as He sat 'enthroned between the cherubim' (Exod. 25:22; Ps. 80:1). Placed in front of the ark were the golden pot of manna and the rod of Aaron which had blossomed (Exod. 16:33; Num. 17:10). Apparently they were at a later time placed inside it (Heb. 9:4). But certainly the ark contained the two tablets of the Ten Commandments, symbolizing the gracious covenant and the law.[6]

The apostle John employed the tabernacle as a whole to emphasize that the Second Person of the Godhead, even the Word of God, visibly 'tabernacled' (*eskēnōsen*) among us as a man in the person of the Lord Jesus Christ (John 1:14).[7] Indeed, some Johannine scholars suggest that a parallel exists between the order of the furnishings of the tabernacle and the arrangement of the Gospel material itself. For after informing his readers that the Word 'tabernacled' among men, by having John the Baptist twice bid his disciples:

---

[6]Gleason L. Archer, Jr., *A Survey of Old Testament Introduction* (Revised and expanded edition; Chicago: Moody, 1964), 254-55.

[7]Leon Morris, *The Gospel According to John* (Grand Rapids: Eerdmans, 1971) writes: 'That John means [by his verb "tabernacled" for] us to recall God's presence in the tabernacle in the wilderness seems clear from the immediate reference to "glory", for glory was associated with the tabernacle' (103).

'Behold the Lamb of God' (John 1:29, 36) John leads them to the brazen altar of sacrifice.

In John 3–4 he takes them to the laver, telling them that except a man be born of water and of the Spirit he cannot enter the kingdom of God (John 3:6) and that if a man will drink of the living water that he gives he shall never thirst again (John 4:14).

In John 6 he leads them to the table of the bread of the presence by informing them that Jesus is the living Bread (John 6:35, 51).

In John 8–9 he takes them to the lampstand, telling them that Jesus 'is the Light of the world; he who follows [him] shall not walk in the darkness but shall have the light of life' (John 8:12; see also 9:5).

Then in John 14–17 they find themselves at the altar of incense where they learn that they are to pray in Jesus' name. Then by Jesus' high priestly prayer in John 17 John takes them behind the veil into the Most Holy Place where they hear their high priest interceding for them in the presence of God.

In John 19 as they gaze on Christ hanging on the cross they behold the true and antitypical propitiatory blood covering the ark of the covenant where their atonement was finally, once and for all, accomplished.

Finally, the symbolic meaning of the Shekinah glory that took up its abode in the tabernacle (Exod. 40:34-35) is disclosed in John 20:22 when Jesus breathed upon his disciples and said to them: 'Receive the Holy Spirit.'

THE AARONIC PRIESTHOOD (EXOD. 28–29, 39; LEV. 8–9)

Aaron, Moses' brother, was divinely chosen to be Israel's first high priest and he served in that office nearly forty years. When the tabernacle was completed Aaron and his sons were set apart to the priesthood by washing to signify purification, by official clothing for beauty and glory, and by anointing with oil to picture the need of empowering by the Holy Spirit (Exod. 28; 40:12-15). Aaron died at the age of 123 on Mt. Hor after Moses had removed his elaborate priestly garments and put them on Aaron's son Eleazar (Num. 20:23-29; 33:38-39). And because the priest's office was hereditary and inherited, all subsequent priests after Aaron had to trace their ancestry back to him. Moreover, no one was to enter the Most Holy Place except the high priest on the Day of Atonement (Lev. 16; Num. 16:39-40; 17:1-11).

Concerning the Aaronic priesthood as an institution and its numerous offerings prescribed by the Levitical legislation the Author of Hebrews declares that this priestly system was superseded and rendered obsolete by the priestly order of Melchizedek (Heb. 8:13) that

- is founded on a 'better covenant' (Heb. 7:22) and 'better promises' (Heb. 8:6),
- introduces a 'better hope' (Heb. 7:19), and
- serves 'the greater and more perfect tabernacle that is not man-made' (Heb. 9:11) with 'better sacrifices' (Heb. 9:23).

Why is this? Because Jesus Christ is the divine High Priest after the order of Melchizedek whose one all-sufficient sacrifice of himself is efficacious for his people for all time to come! Christ's Lamb work as the Priest after the order of Melchizedek satisfied divine justice *once for all* with respect to the sins of all those for whom he died, as witnessed by Holy Scripture and by the fact that God raised him from the dead. *His* sacrifice requires no repetition:

- 'The death he died, he died to sin *once for all* [*ephapax*]' (Rom. 6:10).
- 'Unlike the other high priests, he does not need to offer sacrifices day after day…. He sacrificed for their sins *once for all* [*ephapax*] when he offered himself' (Heb. 7:27).
- 'He did not enter by means of the blood of goats and calves; but he entered the Most Holy Place *once for all* [*ephapax*] by his own blood, having obtained eternal redemption' (Heb. 9:12).
- 'Nor did he enter heaven to offer himself again and again … now he has appeared *once for all* [*hapax*] at the end of the ages to do away with sin by the sacrifice of himself … so Christ was sacrificed *once for all* [*hapax*] to take away the sins of many people' (Heb. 9:25-26, 28).
- '…we have been made holy through the sacrifice of the body of Jesus Christ *once for all* [*ephapax*]. Day after day every priest stands and performs his religious duties; again and again he offers the same sacrifices that can never take away sins. But when this priest had offered *for all time* [*eis to diēnekes*] one sacrifice for sins, he sat down at the right hand of God. Since that time he waits for his enemies to be made his footstool, because by one sacrifice he has made perfect forever those who are being made holy' (Heb. 10:10-14).

- The Author of Hebrews then informs us that once we have received the forgiveness of sins by Christ's 'once for all time' sacrifice, 'there is no longer any sacrifice for sins' (Heb. 10:18).
- 'For Christ died for sins *once for all* [*hapax*], the righteous for the unrighteous, to bring us to God' (1 Pet. 3:18).

The Author of Hebrews drives this point home by comparing the two priestly systems of Holy Scripture:

- 'If perfection could have been attained through the Levitical priesthood…, why was there still need for another priest to come – one in the order of Melchizedek and not in the order of Aaron?' (Heb. 7:11).
- '…the ministry Jesus has received is as superior to [the Aaronic ministry] as the covenant of which he is mediator is superior to the old one…. For if there had been nothing wrong with that first covenant, no place would have been sought for another' (Heb. 8:6-7).
- '…the gifts and sacrifices being offered [in the Aaronic order] were not able to clear the conscience of the worshiper… [their offerings made the worshiper only] outwardly clean. How much more, then, will the blood of Christ … cleanse our consciences from acts that lead to death, so that we may serve the living God?' (Heb. 9:9, 13-14).
- '[The Aaronic sacrifices that can never take away sin, Heb. 10:11] can never … perfect those who draw near to worship…. But when [Christ] had offered for all time [*eis to diēnekes*] one sacrifice for sins, he sat down at the right hand of God … because by one sacrifice he has made perfect forever those who are being made holy' (Heb. 10:1, 12, 14).

From these biblical notices it is indisputable that the tabernacle and the Levitical protocols that the Aaronic priesthood conducted there gave way in due course, as type and shadow give away to antitype and substance, to Jesus Christ's high priestly ministry conducted after the order of Melchizedek.

Jesus Christ, being 'holy, blameless, pure, set apart from sinners, exalted above the heavens' (Heb. 7:26), is the *only* high priest in the order of Melchizedek,

- who as such is a priest *forever* (Heb. 5:6; 6:20; 7:3, 17, 21),
- who possesses an '*indestructible* life' (Heb. 7:16) and a '*permanent* priesthood' (Heb. 7:24),
- who is 'able to save *completely* those who come to God through him because he *always* lives to intercede for them' (Heb. 7:25), and
- who, unlike the high priest of the Aaronic order, 'does not need to offer sacrifices day after day, first for his own sins, and then for the sins of the people' since 'he sacrificed for their sins *once for all* when he offered himself' (Heb. 7:27-28), that is, when 'he entered the Most Holy Place *once for all* by his own blood, having obtained *eternal* redemption' (Heb. 9:12).

When, where, and how did his entrance into the Most Holy Place occur? George Eldon Ladd is correct, in my opinion, when he states:

…the tabernacle with its priests was a copy and shadow of the heavenly sanctuary. *The real has come to men in the historical life and death of Jesus of Nazareth.* History has become the medium of the eternal….

To be sure, Hebrews represents Christ as entering into the Holy Place in heaven, taking his own blood (9:12): However, it is difficult to think that the author of Hebrews conceived of Jesus after his ascension realistically entering a literal Holy Place in heaven. To be sure, he does say, 'Thus it was necessary for the copies of the heavenly things to be purified with these [animal] rites, but the heavenly things themselves with better sacrifices than these' (9:23). [But] it is self-evident that the heavenly things experience no defilement or sin and therefore require no cleansing…. [And the heavenly things do not need *multiple* 'sacrifices' to be made – RLR.] A statement like this should make it clear that Hebrews is describing heavenly things in earthly, symbolic language. What Christ did at the cross, although an event in space and time, was itself an event in the spiritual world. Eternity at this point intersects time; the heavenly is embodied in the earthly; the transcendental occurs in the historical. Christ's entrance into the Holy Place and [his] sprinkling of his blood to effect cleansing and an eternal salvation occurred when 'he … appeared once for all at the end of the age to put away sin by the sacrifice of himself' (9:26). Christ offered himself on the cross to purify his people (9:14). Sanctification was secured when Jesus sacrificed his body 'once for all' (10:10). By dying, he 'offered for all time a single sacrifice for sins' (10:12). Hebrews uses the liturgical language of the Old Testament [priestly] cult to depict the spiritual meaning of what Jesus accomplished by his death on the cross. Here in history on earth is no shadow, but the very reality itself.[8]

In other words, Christ's 'entrance into the heavenly sanctuary' occurred when he assumed his high priestly role as Mediator of the new covenant, and the Most Holy Place was his cross! Therefore, there is no further need for an earthly priesthood to continue to offer sacrifices to God, either animal or human. What Christ, our heavenly High Priest, has done is to make his people – *all* of them – 'priests to serve his God and Father' (Rev. 1:6; 5:10; 20:6), indeed, he has made them all a 'holy priesthood, offering spiritual sacrifices acceptable to God through Jesus Christ' (1 Pet. 2:5) and a 'royal priesthood' that they 'may declare the praises of him who called [them] out of darkness into his wonderful light' (1 Pet. 2:9). Such people need no other priest before God than the one high priest Jesus Christ who is the propitiation for their sins and their Advocate before the Father who sits at the Father's right hand (1 John 2:1-2). If ministers of the gospel have a 'priestly duty' in this present age – and they surely do – it is the 'priestly duty' about which Paul writes in Romans 15:16, namely, the 'duty of proclaiming the gospel of God, so that the Gentiles might become an offering acceptable to God, sanctified by the Holy Spirit' (see Isa. 66:20). Charles Hodge correctly observes on Romans 15:16:

> In this beautiful passage we see the nature of the only priesthood which belongs to the Christian ministry. It is not their office to make atonement for sin, or to offer a propitiatory sacrifice to God, but by the preaching of the gospel to bring men, by the influence of the Holy Spirit, to offer themselves as a living sacrifice, holy and acceptable to God. It is well worthy of remark, that amidst the numerous designations of the ministers of the gospel in the New Testament, intended to set forth the nature of their office, they are never officially called priests. *This is the only passage in which the term is even figuratively applied to them*, and that under circumstances which render its misapprehension impossible. They are not mediators between God and man; they do not offer propitiatory sacrifices. Their only priesthood, as Theophylact says, is the preaching of the gospel, … and their offerings are redeemed and sanctified men, saved by their instrumentality.[9]

---

[8]George Eldon Ladd, *A Theology of the New Testament* (Grand Rapids: Eerdmans, 1974), 574-75 (emphasis original).

[9]Charles Hodge, *Commentary on the Epistle to the Romans* (Reprint of revised 1886 edition; Grand Rapids: Eermans, 1955), 439 (emphasis supplied).

Is it any wonder then that John Calvin declared that Roman Catholicism's priestly system is 'attempting something ingenious: to shape one religion out of Christianity and Judaism[10] and paganism [he refers here to Rome's fiction of transubstantiation and the concomitant adoration of created things] by sewing patches together.'[11] The unscriptural Roman priesthood as it goes about its offerings of an 'unbloody sacrifice' in its myriad Masses offered daily, states Calvin, blasphemes Christ, suppresses the eternal power of his Lamb work to save sinners once and for all, wipes out the true and unique death of Christ, robs men of the benefit of his death, and nullifies the true significance of the Lord's Supper.[12]

---

[10]In spite of the insistence of the Author of Hebrews (Paul?) that Christ's priesthood after the order of Melchizedek superseded and rendered null and void the Aaronic priesthood, Rome declares that the Aaronic order is still normative and that its priests serve in the Aaronic order. I would ask the Roman priest: 'Is the "bloodless sacrifice" you make in the Mass perfect or imperfect?' If he says it is perfect then he must be able to explain, first, how it is that he, an Aaronic priest, has a perfect sacrifice to offer when Aaron himself, the head of his order, never had such a sacrifice; and second, why he needs to continue to offer it if it is perfect. If he says it is imperfect then he must be able to explain, first, why he is offering it since it is incapable of clearing the conscience or perfecting those who attempt to come to God by it; and second, how it is that his 'unbloody' sacrifice can take away sin when 'without the shedding of blood there is no forgiveness' (Heb. 9:22). If he should attempt the impossible and say that he is also serving in the order of Melchizedek then it must be said that he serves in a priestly order created out of whole cloth that has no scriptural warrant whatever.

[11]John Calvin, *Institutes of the Christian Religion*, 4.19.31.

[12]Calvin, *Institutes*, 4.18.2-7.

CHAPTER SIX

THE LAMB CODIFIED:
LEVITICUS 1–7; 16:1-16

Following upon the redemptive event of the Exodus and the legislation related to the paschal lamb and upon the building of the tabernacle and the consecration of the Aaronic priesthood, Leviticus, the third book of the Law, codified the elaborate protocols of the sacrificial system that the redeemed people of the Exodus were to observe throughout their generations.[1] And they were indeed elaborate. The priestly legislation required the priests to offer a lamb each morning and each evening (Exod. 29:38-42) and on the Sabbath, on special days of religious significance such as the first day of the new month (Num. 28:11), each day of the Passover (Num. 28:16-19), at the Feast of Pentecost (Num. 28:26f), the Feast of Trumpets (Num. 29:1-2), the Day of Atonement (Num. 29:7-8), and the Feast of Tabernacles (Num. 29:12-16). They were also to sacrifice a lamb on special occasions, for example, in order to cleanse a woman after giving birth (Lev. 12:6) and when a leper was cleansed (Lev. 14:10-18).

Gleason Archer lays out the several types of blood sacrifices in the Levitical legislation and distinguishes between them in the following ways:[2]

---

[1]Regrettably, Vos, *Biblical Theology*, 173, contends: '…the Pentateuch contains no record of the institution of sacrifice either as to its expiatory or as to its consecratory aspect.' But what is Leviticus if it is not a 'record of the institution of sacrifice'? What is the Passover legislation in Exodus 12 if it is not a 'record of the institution of sacrifice'? And what is Genesis 3:21 if it is not a 'record of the institution of sacrifice'? Surely we see sacrifice for sin instituted in these contexts! One has to conclude that when Vos wrote this absurd statement it was a case of 'Homer nodding'!

[2]Archer, *A Survey of Old Testament Introduction*, 262.

- The burnt offering (*'ōlāh*) made atonement for sin in general and served as a means of approach by an unholy people to the holy God. It was to be an unblemished male ox, sheep, goat, or dove (according to the offerer's wealth), belonged entirely to God, and was to be consumed entirely on the altar (hence it was also called *kālîl*, 'whole burnt offering'). Neither the priest nor the offerer was to eat any portion of it.
- The sin offering (*hattā'th*) made atonement for specific transgressions where no restitution was possible. It was to be a bullock for the priest and the congregation, a male goat for a ruler and a female goat for a commoner. The fatty portions covering the innards, kidney, liver, and caul belonged to God and were to be consumed on the altar. The priests were to eat all the rest within the outer court of the tabernacle. The offerer was to eat no portion of it.
- The trespass offering (*'āshām*) made atonement for specific transgressions where restitution was possible with damages computed at six-fifths payable in advance. It was to be a ram. The fatty portions covering the innards, kidney, liver, and caul belonged to God and were to be consumed on the altar. The priests were to eat all the rest within the outer court of the tabernacle. The offerer was to eat no portion of it.

There were three types of peace offerings (*shelāmîm*):

- the thankoffering (*tôdāh*) as a communion meal was for fellowship with God and for unexpected blessing or deliverance already granted. It was to be an unblemished male or female ox, sheep, or goat. The fatty portions belonged to God. As a wave offering the breast belonged to the high priest, as a heave offering the right foreleg belonged to the officiating priest. These parts could be eaten in any clean place. The remainder was to be eaten in the outer court the same day.
- the votive offering (*nēdher*) as a communion meal was for blessing and deliverance already granted, with a vow to be made in support of any petition. It was to be an unblemished male or female ox, sheep, or goat. The fatty portions belonged to God. As a wave offering the breast belonged to the high priest, as a heave offering

the right foreleg belonged to the officiating priest. These parts could be eaten in any clean place. The remainder was to be eaten in the outer court the same day.

- the free will offering (*nedhābhāh*) as a communion meal expressed general thankfulness and love toward God without regard to specific blessings. It was to be a male or female ox, sheep, or goat (minor imperfections were permitted). The fatty portions belonged to God. As a wave offering the breast belonged to the high priest, as a heave offering the right foreleg belonged to the officiating priest. These parts could be eaten in any clean place. The remainder was to be eaten in the outer court on that or the succeeding day.

Today this legislation seems to the Western mind unschooled in biblical matters to be barbaric, overly technical, and complicated, but by this legislation God was schooling Israel in the great principle of forgiveness through the substitutionary death of an innocent sacrifice for the guilty. Again and again in that body of legislative material the guilty Israelite is instructed to 'lay his hand on the head of the [unblemished] burnt offering' and was told that 'it will be accepted on his behalf to make atonement for him (Lev. 1:4; 3:2, 8, 13; 4:4, 15, 24, 29, 33; Num. 8:12). The salvific significance of this ritual was not left to the speculative mind to decipher but was clearly explained in connection with the activity of the Day of Atonement (*yôm kippûr*) – the centerpiece of the Levitical legislation – described in Leviticus 16.

Once a year, on the Day of Atonement, the high priest chose two goats. He sacrificed one of them for a sin offering and took its blood and sprinkled it on the mercy seat inside the Most Holy Place, then on the furniture inside the Holy Place, and then on the Brazen Altar. Then he was to take the live goat, the so-called 'scapegoat,' 'lay both hands on the head of the live goat and confess over it all the wickedness and rebellion of the Israelites – all their sins – and *put them on the goat's head*, and send the goat away into the desert.... The goat will *carry on itself* all their sins to a solitary place...' (Lev. 16:21-22). By this ritual the great salvific principle was being taught that salvation comes to the sinner who turns for forgiveness away from his own efforts, who approaches God through the blood sacrifice offered in his stead, and whose sins are imputed to that substitutionary sacrifice. Of course, the type finds its *exclusive* antitype in the substitutionary Lamb work of Jesus Christ.

J. I. Packer quite properly understands the activity regarding the so-called 'scapegoat' as a 'dramatization' of what occurred in the sacrifice of the *other* goat:

> The [other] goat is the one that really counts. The action with the scapegoat is only a picture of what happens through the [other] goat. The [other] goat is killed and offered as a sin-offering in the normal way. Thus atonement was made for the people of Israel. The banishing of the scapegoat into the wilderness was an illustrative device to make plain to God's people that their sin really has been taken away.
>
> When the writer of Hebrews speaks of Christ achieving what the Day of Atonement typified [Heb. 9:11-14] – our perfect and permanent cleansing from sin – he focuses not on the goat that went away into the wilderness but on the animal that was offered in sacrifice once a year by the high priest … the blood of Christ [fulfills] the whole pattern of the Day of Atonement ritual.[3]

All this raises the question that must be asked and answered: 'Were these animal sacrifices in and of themselves the ground for the forgiveness of sin?' The answer, to be biblical, must be a resounding 'No.' *Not one had any intrinsic capability to take away sin!* The Author of Hebrews could hardly be more explicit here:

- '…the gifts and sacrifices being offered [by the Aaronic priests under the Levitical system] were not able to clear the conscience of the worshiper … [their offerings made the worshiper only] outwardly clean' (Heb. 9:9, 13-14).
- 'It was necessary … for the copies of the heavenly things [that is, the wilderness tabernacle and its furnishings] to be purified with these sacrifices, but [it was necessary for] the heavenly things themselves [to be purified] with *better sacrifices than these* [that is, with the one all-sufficient sacrifice of Christ that fulfills the entire range of Old Testament sacrifices]' (Heb. 9:23 24).
- 'The law is only a shadow of the good things that are coming – not the realities themselves. For this reason it can never, by the same sacrifices repeated endlessly year after year make perfect those who

---

[3]J. I. Packer, 'Sacrifice and Satisfaction,' in *Our Savior God: Man, Christ, and the Atonement*, edited by James M. Boice (Grand Rapids: Baker, 1980), 131-32.

draw near to worship … *because it is impossible for the blood of bulls
and goats to take away sins*…. Day after day every priest stands and
performs his religious duties; again and again he offers the same
sacrifices, which can never take away sins' (Heb. 10:1, 4, 11).

And yet the same Author insists: '…without the shedding of blood there is
no forgiveness' (Heb. 9:22). So what does this all mean? How do we make
sense of all this? *Westminster Confession of Faith*, 7.5 helps us here by informing
us that the Old Testament sacrifices were teaching tools in the hand of the
Holy Spirit whereby the elect of God were taught to trust in the coming
Messiah's Lamb work that they all foresignified:

> …under the law [the covenant of grace] was administered by promises,
> prophecies, sacrifices, circumcision, the paschal lamb, and other types and
> ordinances delivered to the people of the Jews, *all foresignifying Christ to come*;
> which were, for the time, sufficient and efficacious, through the operation of
> the Spirit, to instruct and build up the elect in faith in the promised Messiah,
> by whom they had full remission of sins, and eternal salvation….[4]

Westminster Confession of Faith, 8.6 makes the same point, albeit in a more
direct soteric setting and in different words, when it declares:

> Although the work of redemption was not actually wrought by Christ till
> after His incarnation, yet the virtue, efficacy, and benefits thereof were
> communicated unto the elect, in all ages successively from the beginning
> of the world, *in and by those promises, types, and sacrifices, where He was revealed,*
> and signified to be the seed of the woman which should bruise the serpent's
> head, and the Lamb slain from the beginning of the world; being yesterday
> and today the same, and forever.

Thus the Levitical system foreshadowed the sacrificial work of Jesus Christ
who saved the elect in Israel as they placed their trust in him as he was
foresignified by the earthly types within that sacrificial system. In other

---

[4]Contrary to Dallas Seminary dispensationalism the Old Testament saints through
the work of God's Spirit in them by means of the 'promises, prophecies, sacrifices,
circumcision, the paschal lamb, and other types and ordinances' learned that Messiah's
ministry would have a 'suffering' dimension to it. For full discussion of this controversy
see my *A New Systematic Theology of the Christian Faith*, 503-35.

words, while the Old Testament sacrifices had no intrinsic power in themselves to save, they became as types of Christ's Lamb work sufficient and efficacious instrumentalities through the Holy Spirit's saving operation in the hearts of God's elect to turn them away from their own efforts in self-salvation and to build up their faith in the 'Lamb work' of the promised Messiah who granted them full remission of sins and eternal salvation. Isaac Watts put it this way in verse:

> Not all the blood of beasts on Jewish altars slain,
> Could give the guilty conscience peace, or wash away the stain.
> But Christ, the heavenly Lamb, takes all our sins away,
> A sacrifice of nobler name and richer blood than they.

What must be clearly understood by this is that the *entire* sacrificial system of the Old Testament had meaning, efficacy, and value only because it typically pointed forward to the sacrifice of the sinless Messiah on Calvary as the antitypical Lamb of God. *Not to relate, as type to antitype, the earlier Levitical legislation to the 'Lamb work' of Christ is to decapitate that legislation and empty it of any significance!* Indeed, it is not going too far to say that if the typical Old Testament sacrificial system does not find its divinely intended antitypical fulfillment in the death of Jesus Christ in the New Testament, two conclusions must inevitably follow: First, the priestly cultus in Israel was simply reflecting the barbarous cultic thinking of the ancient Near East in general during the mid-second-millennium B.C. Second, Moses, the giver of this legislation, far from being the world's greatest lawgiver, as he is commonly touted to be, was actually one of the greatest barbarians who ever lived, for by his priestly legislation he started a fourteen-hundred-year-long river of animal blood flowing at altar, tabernacle and temple and placed human armies on ancient battlefields to protect and perpetuate this legislation for posterity.

Chapter Seven

The Lamb Deified:
Isaiah 7:14-16; 9:6-7

The history of redemptive revelation after the Mosaic age continued to unfold through the United Kingdom Period when Solomon's Temple was built in Jerusalem and into the Divided Kingdom Period. In the eighth century God called the prophet Isaiah whom Gleason L. Archer, Jr. labels 'the evangelical prophet' because he 'sets forth the doctrine of Christ in such full detail.... Deeper Christological insights are to be found in his work than anywhere else in the Old Testament.'[1] With the exception, perhaps, of some of the messianic psalms of David, surely he is right. Isaiah's prophecy of the *'almah*, who would conceive and bear a son who would be Immanuel (7:14-16) is a classic case in point.

It is true that the word 'Lamb' does not occur in the contexts of Isaiah 7:14 and 9:6, but in light of the larger context of Isaiah's messianic teaching it is plain that the subject of his discourses in these two passages is the Servant-Lamb of Isaiah 53:7. Therefore, in order to treat the antitypical Lamb's divine nature I will say something about these earlier statements in Isaiah's prophecy.

Isaiah 7:14-16

The historical setting of the prophecy
The prophecy's historical setting is well known. During the reign of King Ahaz of Judah, probably around 734 BC, Rezin, king of Syria, and Pekah, king of Israel, formed an alliance against Ahaz of Judah to dethrone him and

---

[1]Archer, *A Survey of Old Testament Introduction*, 363.

to install in his place the son of Tabeel as a puppet king who would do their bidding and bring Judah into their coalition against Assyria.[2] News of their alliance produced great anxiety throughout the southern kingdom of Judah, so God sent Isaiah to Ahaz to assure him that the plot against him would come to nought. But as a warning to Ahaz not to rely on an alliance of his own with Assyria (see 7:9), God informed him that within sixty-five years the northern kingdom, in spite of its Syrian alliance, would be 'broken'. We may note here that, historically, the alliance was 'broken' in three stages: Assyria overran Damascus and despoiled the northern kingdom in 732 BC (2 Kgs. 15:29), then Samaria fell to the Assyrians in 722 BC, and finally, with the Assyrians' deportation of the Israelite population and the colonization of the land with non-Israelites (see 2 Kgs. 17:24ff. and Ezra 4:2, 10), by 669 BC (sixty-five years from 734 BC), when Ashurbanipal began to reign over Assyria, Ephraim's destruction became complete.[3]

To give a pointed lesson to the faithless Ahaz that he should put his confidence in God and not in Assyria, and also to encourage him to do so, God graciously invited Ahaz to ask him for a 'sign' ('ōth) as a confirmation or attestation of his power to save Judah. Ahaz was informed, in so many words, that he was not to feel the slightest restriction in what he could request, for he was granted unfettered latitude of request 'whether in the deepest depth or in the highest heights'. Any righteous request within the bounds of this antonymic venue, which is just to say any righteous request at all, was permissible.

Since it has often been suggested that the word 'sign' in 7:14 does not mean that the thing it signified should be understood as necessarily entailing something out of the ordinary, I think it important to stress here that at least in Isaiah 7:11 it is quite apparent that it was precisely the 'extraordinary' or the 'miraculous' that God had in mind when he extended to Ahaz his invitation. And had Ahaz requested of him a miracle, God was prepared to perform one. This is evident from the proximate purpose that the sign was to serve (a proof that God was able to deliver and to keep his people) and

---

[2] See Edward J. Young, 'The Immanuel Prophecy,' in *Studies in Isaiah* (London: Tyndale, 1954), 145-48, for a reconstruction of the historical background to the prophecy in which reconstruction he harmonizes the details of 2 Kings 15:37; 16:1-9; 2 Chronicles 28:5-21; and Isaiah 7:1-9.

[3] This is essentially the view of Gleason L. Archer, Jr., as well. See his 'Isaiah,' in *The Wycliffe Bible Commentary*, edited by C. F. Pfeiffer and E. F. Harrison (Chicago: Moody, 1962), 617.

from the unrestricted latitude in the invitation that was extended to Ahaz. It is not too much to say that upon this occasion God was 'thinking miracle' and was ready to perform one as a sign to Ahaz of the certainty of his promise. So while it does not prove that the sign spoken of in verses 14-16 must be construed as entailing the miraculous, the fact that the referent of the word 'sign' in verse 11 clearly is of that order lends strong credence to the presumption that, when God declared in verse 14 that he himself would give a 'sign' since Ahaz had refused to ask for one, the words that then followed upon his declaration that he would give a 'sign' also entailed the miraculous.

Ahaz, because he had doubtless already determined to rely upon a coalition with Assyria (see 2 Kgs. 16:5-9), feigned great piety and refused God's gracious invitation, hypocritically declaring that to ask for a sign was to test God (an appeal to Deut. 6:16). At this, God declared that he himself would give a sign – not only to Ahaz but also to the whole House of David – implying by this latter statement that the sign carried implications for the entire nation and for its future. God's sign is then stated in these verses (7:14-16):

> Behold, the *'almah* [that is, the specific one before the prophet's mind in his vision] is [or, will be] with child and will give birth to a son and will call[4] his name Immanuel. Curds and honey he will eat when he knows enough to reject the wrong and choose the right. For before the child knows enough to reject the wrong and choose the right, the land which you dread will be forsaken of her two kings.

---

[4] I regard the verb *wᵉqārāth* of the MT as a *third* feminine singular ('and *she* will call') that is supported by the *kalesei* in a in spite of the fact that it has the appearance of a *second* feminine singular that is supported by the *kaleseis* in A and B. Some scholars (see Walter C. Kaiser, Jr., *Toward an Old Testament Theology* [Grand Rapids: Zondervan, 1978], 208) stress that the verb should be construed as a second feminine singular ('and *you*, the *'almāh*, will call'), and that it indicates that the *'almāh* was standing before the prophet as he spoke. But *Gesenius' Hebrew Grammar* (Corrected second English edition; Oxford: Clarendon, 1910) explains this particular form as a 'rarer form' of the *third* feminine singular in *lamedh 'aleph* verbs (see 120, par. 44f, 206, par. 74g). Besides, Matthew's citation of Isaiah 7:14 reads *kalesousin* ('and *they* will call'), the third common *plural* form, suggesting, to say the least, that in the final analysis precisely who it was who would actually do the 'naming' apparently is of no great moment. The verb form simply cannot support the exegetical freight that these scholars want it to carry.

THE MEANING AND REFERENT OF THE '*ALMAH*

What does *'almah* mean here, and to whom does it refer? These questions have received many responses. Two such studies of this word were conducted by Robert Dick Wilson and Edward J. Young, in which the nine occurrences of the word in the Old Testament (five times in the plural – Song of Solomon 1:3; 6:8; Psalm 46, superscription; 68:25 (MT, v. 26); 1 Chronicles 15:20; four times in the singular – Genesis 24:43; Exodus 2:8; Proverbs 30:19; Isaiah 7:14) were investigated (1) contextually, (2) against their historical background, and (3) in the versions, including in the case of Young's study a consideration of the Ras Shamra material from ancient Ugarit. Both came to the same conclusion: *never is the word employed to describe a married woman*. Their conclusions are worthy of quotation. Robert Dick Wilson wrote:

> ...two conclusions from the evidence seem clear; first, that *'alma*, so far as known, never meant 'young married woman'; and secondly since the presumption in common law and usage was and is, that every *'alma* is virgin and virtuous, until she is proven not to be, we have a right to assume that Rebecca and the *'alma* of Is. vii. 14 and all other *'almas* were virgin, until and unless it shall be proven that they were not.[5]

E. J. Young's conclusion is similar:

> We are far from asserting that this word is the precise equivalent of the English 'virgin.' It rather seems to be closer to words such as 'damsel' or 'maiden', words which most naturally suggest an unmarried girl. In fact the Hebrew word *'almah* would seem to be a shade stronger than the English words 'maiden' and 'damsel', since there is no evidence that it was ever used of a married woman. Consequently, one is tempted to wish that those who repeat the old assertion that it may be used of a woman, whether married or not, would produce some evidence for their statement.
>
> In the light of this fact that the word is never used of a married woman, and in the light of the Ras Shamra texts, where it is found as a practical synonym of *bethulah* ['virgin'], both words there referring to an unmarried goddess, we believe that the translators of the Septuagint brought out the true force of the passage when they rendered the word by *he parthenos* ['virgin'].[6]

---

[5]Robert Dick Wilson, 'The Meaning of 'Alma (A.V. 'Virgin') in Isaiah VII. 14,' in *Princeton Theological Review* XXIV (1926), 316.

In my opinion, Matthew, guided by the Holy Spirit, had already placed the validity of their shared conclusion beyond all doubt when he declared (1) that the Lord meant 'virgin' when he said what he did to Ahaz, and (2) that Jesus' miraculous conception and birth were the fulfillment of Isaiah's prophecy:

> All this took place to fulfill what the Lord had said through the prophet: 'The virgin will conceive and give birth to a son, and they will call him Immanuel' – which means, 'God with us' (Matt. 1:22-23).

If Matthew is following the LXX here, as many scholars urge, an interesting feature of the LXX translation is that it reflects the *pre-Christian Jewish interpretation* of Isaiah 7:14. It is simply not the case, as some modern Jewish scholars have maintained, that the original reading of the LXX was *hē neanis* ('the young woman') rather than *hē parthenos* ('the virgin') and that early Christians tampered with the text by substituting the latter for the former. The truth of the matter is that Aquila, a second-century convert to Judaism, did an independent Greek translation of the Hebrew Bible and deliberately substituted the former for the latter to avoid the Christian interpretation. But the original LXX translators, doing their work two to three centuries before the birth of Christ and knowing nothing of the fulfillment itself, translated *'almah* by *parthenos*, because they were attempting to deliver a competent translation. Cyrus H. Gordon, one of the most knowledgeable Jewish scholars in Mediterranean studies in this generation, acknowledged as much:

> The commonly held view that 'virgin' is Christian, whereas 'young woman' is Jewish is not quite true. The fact is that the Septuagint, which is the Jewish translation made in pre-Christian Alexandria, takes *'almah* to mean 'virgin' here. Accordingly, the New Testament follows Jewish interpretation in Isaiah 7:14.... The aim of this note is ... to call attention to a source that has not been brought into the discussion. From Ugarit of around 1400 BC comes a text celebrating the marriage of the male and female lunar deities [Nikkal and Yarih]. It is there predicted that the goddess will bear a son.... The terminology is remarkably close to that of Isaiah 7:14. However, the Ugaritic statement that the bride will bear a son is fortunately given in parallelistic form; in 77.7 she is called by the exact etymological

---

[6]Young, 'The Immanuel Prophecy,' in *Studies in Isaiah*, 183-84; see also J. Gresham Machen, *The Virgin Birth of Jesus Christ* (New York: Harper and Brothers, 1930), 288.

counterpart of Hebrew *'almah* 'young woman'; in 77.5 she is called by the exact etymological counterpart of Hebrew *betulah* 'virgin.' Therefore, the New Testament rendering of *'almah* as 'virgin' for Isaiah 7:14 rests on the older Jewish interpretation, which in turn is now borne out for *precisely this annunciation formula* by a text that is not only pre-Isaianic but is pre-Mosaic in the form that we now have it on a clay tablet.[7]

Two caveats are necessary here, however. Even though Gordon's remarks support the view that Isaiah 7:14 was regarded by Jewish scholars before the birth of Christ as referring to a *virgin* birth, the reader must be cautioned not to follow Gordon in his implied suggestion that the New Testament *via Isaiah* is simply reflecting an ancient pagan annunciation formula used to announce the birth of gods and kings. It may well have been such originally, but in Isaiah, as Young trenchantly notes,

> this formula is lifted from its ancient pagan context and made to introduce the announcement of the birth of one who is truly God and King. No longer must this phrase serve the useless purpose of heralding the birth of beings who had never existed and never would exist. Now, for the first time in its history, it becomes a true 'divine-royal *euangelion* formula'.[8]

Finally, Gordon's last comment implies a post-fifteenth century date for Moses, when in actuality Moses was contemporaneous with the Ugaritic corpus from ancient Ras Shamra.

Now there can be no doubt that Matthew, even granting that he followed the LXX (but only because of the propriety of its translation), intended by *parthenos*, the meaning of 'virgin' (*virgo intacta*). This is clear from his statements on both sides of his citation of the Immanuel prophecy, specifically, his statements 'before they came together' (1:18), 'what is conceived in her is from the Holy Spirit' (1:20), and '[Joseph] had no union with her until she gave birth to a son' (1:25). We conclude, then, at this point in our discussion that God's 'sign' to the House of David entailed the announcement that a virgin would both conceive and *while still a virgin* bring forth a son – definitely a miracle and answering thereby the demands of the

---

[7]Cyrus H. Gordon, ' *'Almah* in Isaiah 7:14,' in *The Journal of Bible and Religion* XXI, 2 (April 1953): 106.

[8]Edward J. Young, 'The Immanuel Prophecy,' in *Studies in Isaiah*, 160; see Luke 1:31 for the *final* occurrence of the formula in Gabriel's 'birth annunciation.'

implied meaning in the word 'sign' which was God's characterization of the future event. This interpretation necessarily eliminates as referents of the *'almah*, both Ahaz's wife, whom Vriezen and Kaiser suggest,[9] and Isaiah's own wife (see 7:3, 8:3-4 for the evidence that Isaiah was married), as Archer has urged.

The predicted virginal conception, however, does not exhaust the miraculous features of the sign, for it is apparent, if the mother was to conceive virginally, that the Child, having no biological father, while certainly human would himself necessarily be *unique*. Young aptly comments: 'The emphasis which has been placed upon the mother of the child leads one to the conclusion that the child himself is unusual.'[10] Of course, the direction in which the text itself prompts one to look for help in apprehending the nature of his uniqueness is toward the name he was to be given – Immanuel. What does this name tell us about his character?

The Hebrew *'immānû ʾēl* (Gr. *emmanuel*), meaning 'With us [is] God,' occurs only three times in the Bible as a proper name (Isa. 7:14; 8:8; Matt. 1:23) and, I would urge, it is the name of the same person.[11] Now

---

[9]Th. C. Vriezen, *An Outline of Old Testament Theology* (Newton, Mass.: Charles T. Branford, 1958), 360, fn. 1; Walter C. Kaiser, Jr., *Toward an Old Testament Theology*, 209-10; see also Kaiser's article, 'The Promise of Isaiah 7:14 and the Single-Meaning Hermeneutic,' in *Evangelical Bulletin* 6 (1988), 55-70. In his treatment of the passage Kaiser urges specifically that the *'almâh*, was Abi (a variant form of Abijah), daughter of Zechariah and wife of Ahaz (2 Kgs. 18:2), and that the Immanuel child was Hezekiah. But this cannot be, since, as Kaiser himself recognizes (but discounts because of dating problems surrounding the latter's reign), 'on present chronologies [Hezekiah] must have been nine [*sic*] years old at that time (about 734 BC)' (209). Actually, in my opinion, Hezekiah may have been around nineteen years old in 734 BC, coming to the throne as he apparently did in 728/27 BC at the age of twenty-five (see 2 Kgs. 18:1-2, 9, 10). The reference to his 'fourteenth year' in 2 Kings 18:13 may refer to the fourteenth year of the special fifteen-year dispensation of *additional* life that God granted him (see 2 Kgs. 20:1-11). This would be 701 BC, the year that Old Testament scholars assert was the year in which Sennacherib invaded Judah.

[10]Young, 'The Immanuel Prophecy,' in *Studies in Isaiah*, 194.

[11]The occurrence of *'immānû ʾēl*, in Isaiah 8:10, following as it does the Hebrew particle *kî*, 'for', should be taken as a statement and not as a proper name; that is to say, the clause should be rendered 'for God is [shall be] with us' rather than 'for – [I am] Immanuel!' Therefore, I will not lay any weight upon it in the present discussion except to say that it is an obvious play on the proper name in 8:8 and gives the reason why Assyria's impending devastation of Judah would not prove to be ultimately fatal for Immanuel's land – 'for God [in the person of *'immānû ʾēl*] is with us.'

it does not do justice to the virginally conceived child's uniqueness among men to argue as some do that the name Immanuel was intended merely to symbolize the fact that God was present with the nation in her coming deliverance and nothing more than this. The name by itself, I grant, *might* symbolize nothing more than this, but a *virginally conceived* child who would bear the name 'Immanuel' might well *be* in fact what his name suggests. I say this for the following reasons:

First, in Scripture the name which was given to one (or which one bore) quite often was *descriptive or declarative of what one was* (see, for example, Gen. 17:5, 15-16; 27:36; Exod. 3:13-14; 6:2-3; 1 Sam. 25:25; 2 Sam. 12:25; Matt. 1:21). Just as in Isaiah 4:3 where those who are 'called holy' are not simply *nominally* so but *are in fact* holy (see also Hos. 1:10, Isa. 1:26; Luke 1:31, 35), so also in Isaiah 7:14, to *call* the child 'Immanuel' can and, I would submit, did intend to designate what he would in fact be.

Second, the occurrence of the name in Isaiah suggests that the Child of the Immanuel prophecy was divine. From 8:8 we learn that Immanuel was the *Owner* of the land of Israel, and that he would protect the people of God (see 8:10), clearly implying that the Child would possess divine prerogatives and attributes.

Third, the fact that Matthew 'by-passed' the name 'Jesus' (but see the angel's explanation of 'Jesus' which is reminiscent of Psalm 130:8) which was equally 'un-Greek' and translated 'Immanuel' (the third occurrence of the name) into Greek (1:23) surely suggests, against the background of the angel's earlier statement that 'what is conceived in her is from the Holy Spirit' (1:20), that he intended to teach that in the person of the virginally conceived offspring of Mary God himself had come to dwell with his people *en sarki* ('in flesh') (see Jesus' later promises to *be with his people* in Matthew 18:20 and 28:20).

Fourth, the further descriptions of this Child in Isaiah 9:6 – 'wonderful Counselor, mighty God, everlasting Father, Prince of peace' (not to mention the numerous New Testament applications to Jesus of other descriptions of the Child found in Isaiah 7–12, the so-called 'Volume of Immanuel'[12])

---

[12]For example, (1) the 'Lord of hosts' of Isaiah 8:13 is the 'Lord Christ,' according to 1 Peter 3:14-15; (2) this same 'Lord of hosts' of Isaiah 8:14 who is 'a stone that causes men to stumble and a rock that makes them fall' is the Christ whom the Jews rejected, according to Romans 9:33; (3) and yet he is to be distinguished from the Lord in some sense for, according to the Author of Hebrews, it is the Christ who says in Isaiah 8:17:

– indicate, as we shall see shortly, that the Child of the Immanuel prophecy was to be, as virginally conceived, the divine Son of God.

Only such an understanding of the name as we have suggested here, in my opinion, explains the uniqueness of the Child who was to be conceived in the womb of the virgin mother without the benefit of a human biological father. The biblical evidence, in sum, is quite overwhelming in support of this virginally conceived Child being God in the flesh and thus the only rightful bearer of the descriptive name 'Immanuel' – 'With us [is] God!'

Of course, it should be clearly understood that, while the virginal conception is declared by Scripture to be the *means* whereby the Son of God became man and thus entered into the world, nothing that I have said or have intended to say should be construed to suggest that the virginal conception *per se* was the *cause* or source of the deity of Immanuel. Geerhardus Vos has aptly sounded a cautionary note here when he writes:

> ...there is truth in the close connection established between the virgin birth of our Lord and His Deity. It is, however, a mistake to suspend the Deity on the virgin birth as its ultimate source or reason. The impossibility of this appears when we observe that the virgin birth has reference to the human nature of our Lord, and cannot, therefore, without confusion of the two natures, be regarded as the cause of Deity. Being an event in time, the virgin birth cannot be productive of something eternal. To suspend the Deity of

---

'I will put my trust in him' (Heb. 2:13), and who speaks of having received children from the Lord in Isaiah 8:18 (see 'everlasting Father' in Isa. 9:6) (Heb. 2:13); (4) the geographic locale specified in Isaiah 9:1-2 is applied to the locale of Jesus' ministry in Matthew 4:13-16; (5) the nature of the Child's reign described in Isaiah 9:7 is the background to Gabriel's statement in Luke 1:32-33; (6) the statement that only a remnant in Israel rely upon the Lord and return to the mighty God in Isaiah 10:20-23 (see 'mighty God' in Isaiah 9:6), Paul in Romans 9:27-28 applies to the then-current wide-scale rejection of Jesus Christ; and (7) the Root of Jesse to whom the natives will rally in Isaiah 11:10 is the Christ, according to Paul in Romans 15:12. Clearly, the Child of the 'Volume of Immanuel' is Deity incarnate and yet is in some sense to be distinguished from Deity. Only the postulation of the correlative doctrines of the Incarnation and the Trinity can resolve this otherwise clear contradiction. More examples could be given: As a further explication of the content of that one 'more superior name [than "angel"]' of 'Son,' the Author of Hebrews declares that when this Child was born, God commanded that all the angels should worship him (Heb. 1:6; see Deut. 32:43 LXX), and that as God's Son he is himself the 'God' of Psalm 45:6-7 and the 'Lord' of Psalm 102:25-27. Surely he is deity.

Christ on his virgin birth would lead to a lowering of the idea of Deity itself. Yet, the feeling is quite correct that those who deny the supernatural birth are also prone to deny the true Deity of our Lord and His eternal existence with God before the world was. The combination of affirming the true Deity of Christ while denying the fact of His virgin birth is not a normally sane position, but a mere theological oddity.[13]

THE PROBLEM OF RELEVANCE

The major exegetical objection to this interpretation of Isaiah 7:14 is that the prophecy would have had no relevance for Ahaz's day. A 'sign' that was not to be fulfilled for seven and a half centuries, it is often urged, could hardly have been of any value to the House of David in the eighth century BC. This objection is found in both non-evangelical and evangelical studies of the passage. Of course, in the case of the latter, a valiant effort is made so to interpret the passage that it portends a birth in Isaiah's own day *and* the birth of Christ later. For example, William Sanford LaSor has argued that the Hebrew word '*almâh* must be interpreted broadly enough so that, in addition to its ultimate application to the *virgin mother* of Jesus Christ, it may refer penultimately to an earlier *young woman* in Isaiah's day who would conceive and bear a son *by natural means* whose son would bear the name Immanuel and who would thus become a sign of hope to Ahaz of a deliverance which God was to bring to pass within a dozen years.[14]

Archer also understands the Immanuel prophecy in 7:14 as having a dual fulfillment, the typical fulfillment being in Maher-Shalal-Hash-Baz (8:1-4), son of Isaiah, with the antitypical fulfillment being, of course, in Jesus, son of Mary.[15] But in order to justify this interpretation, Archer must postulate, first, that Shear-Jashub (7:3) was Isaiah's son by a previous wife who had died leaving Isaiah a widower, and second, that he was engaged to be married to a prophetess who was at the time of the prophecy and her marriage to Isaiah a virgin but who, of course, would not have been a virgin at the time of her conception and delivery. But both of these features in his interpretation – Isaiah's widower-hood and his engagement to be married again to the virgin prophetess – are pure assumptions since the Scriptures say nothing

---

[13]Geerhardus Vos, *The Self-Disclosure of Jesus* (Reprint; Phillipsburg, New Jersey: Presbyterian and Reformed, 1978), 191, fn. 15.

[14]William Sanford LaSor, 'Isaiah 7:14 – "Young Woman" or "Virgin"?' (Pasadena: privately published, 1952), 8-9.

[15]Archer, 'Isaiah,' in *The Wycliffe Bible Commentary*, 618.

about *two* wives. They are simply assumptions that Archer must necessarily make if he is to hold the dual-fulfillment view.

A careful reading of both Isaiah 7:14 and Matthew 1:22-25 will disclose, however, that the *'almah* was to be a virgin both at the time of her marriage and *at the time of her conception and her delivery*. Consider the following: the *parthenos*, whom Matthew expressly affirms was a 'virgin' (and whom Archer willingly acknowledges was a virgin at the time of the prophecy), both Isaiah and Matthew also represent as the *same* subject who both conceived *and* delivered: '...the *virgin* shall *conceive* and [the virgin shall] *bring forth* a son.' There is no hint that the virginal status of the *parthenos* changed between the description of her as such and the two verbs ('conceive' and 'bring forth') that follow that description. An analogy would be John 1:14 where we are informed that 'the Word *became* flesh and *dwelt* among us.' The Word, evangelicals would argue, without changing into something else and ceasing to be all that he is as the Word *became* flesh. And the same Word is the subject of the next verb 'dwelt' as well. Similarly, the *parthenos*, without ceasing to be a *parthenos*, both conceived and delivered. This is the reason – what other reason can account for it? – that Matthew underscored the truth that Joseph had no sexual relations with Mary until *after* she had given birth to Jesus (1:25). He clearly intimates that Mary's virginity throughout the duration of her pregnancy was vitally necessary as a fulfillment feature of the Isaiah 7:14 statement that he had cited. In my opinion, this fact necessarily eliminates a dual fulfillment for Isaiah 7:14 and requires that the Immanuel prophecy be applied exclusively to Christ. The reader will have to judge whether a woman who would be a virgin at her marriage but not a virgin either at conception or at delivery (that is, the prophetess) could have possibly served as a type of the future antitypical woman who prior to her marriage would still be a virgin both at conception and at delivery (that is, Mary), and whether Isaiah 7:14 can be so read that it allows both of these quite dissimilar situations to fall within the parameters of the linguistic tolerances of the verse. In my opinion, this resort to 'double fulfillment' or 'double meaning,' as J. Barton Payne urges, fails to take seriously the fact that 'the *'alma* of Isa. 7:14 either was a virgin or was not and cannot simultaneously predict these two opposing meanings.'[16] As I have said, it flies in the face of Matthew's assertion that the Immanuel prophecy describes the *'almah*, as a

---

[16]J. Barton Payne, *Encyclopedia of Biblical Prophecy* (New York: Harper and Row, 1973), 292, fn. 61; see also J. A. Alexander, *Isaiah Translated and Explained* (Philadelphia: Presbyterian Board of Publication, 1851), I, 106-07.

virgin *not only at the moment of conception but also throughout her pregnancy up to and including the event of her delivery*.

THE SOLUTION TO THE PROBLEM OF RELEVANCE

What is the solution, then, to the problem of relevance for its contemporaries of a 'sign' prophecy that was not to be fulfilled for seven and a half centuries? At least four solutions have been proposed in response to this objection:

1. Joseph Addison Alexander in his great critical commentary on Isaiah argued that the assurance that Christ was to be born in Judah, of its royal family, might be a *sign* to Ahaz that the kingdom should not perish in his day; and so far was the remoteness of the sign in this case from making it absurd or inappropriate that the further off it was, the stronger the promise of continuance of Judah which it guaranteed.[17] The problem with this response is that it seems to make the relevance of the prophecy turn on the awareness on the part of the original recipients that its fulfillment was to be in the *distant* future.

2. J. Barton Payne, with keener insight, argued that the relevance of the prophecy for the eighth century BC was dependent neither upon the immediacy of its fulfillment nor upon Ahaz's awareness of its distant future fulfillment. A prophecy, he writes,

> may serve as a valid force in motivating conduct [and instilling consolation], irrespective of the interval preceding its historical fulfillment, provided only that the contemporary audience *does not know* when this fulfillment is to take place. Even as the Lord's second coming should motivate our faithful conduct, no matter how distant it may be…, so Isa. 7:14, on His miraculous first coming, was equally valid for motivating Ahaz, 730 years before Jesus' birth.[18]

That is to say, according to Payne, precisely because Ahaz *did not know* when the prophecy would be fulfilled, 'the time lapse need not diminish the contemporary relevance of Isaiah's warning' even though Immanuel was not

---

[17] J. A. Alexander, *The Earlier Prophecies of Isaiah* (New York: Wiley and Putnam, 1846), I, 119; Charles Lee Feinberg, 'The Virgin Birth in the Old Testament and Isaiah 7:14,' in *Bibliotheca Sacra* 119 (1962): 258, also seems to support this proposal.

[18] J. Barton Payne, *Enyclopedia of Biblical Prophecy*, 292, emphasis supplied.

to appear for more than seven centuries.[19] Payne's interesting solution is the antithesis to that proposed by Alexander, inasmuch as Alexander's view looks to the recipients' *awareness* of the prophecy's distant fulfillment as the ground of its relevance whereas Payne's view roots the relevance of the prophecy in the recipients' *lack of awareness* of the time of its fulfillment. Payne's view resolves the difficulty implicit in Alexander's proposal. But his view also appears to cut off from 7:14 the following two verses, verses which as a part of the sign statement seem to provide the very measure of time (in relative terms) between that moment and Judah's subsequent deliverance from the threat from the north which Payne seems to suggest is absent from the passage.

3. As did John Calvin, Robert I. Vasholz attempts to show the relevance of the prophecy by arguing that, while Isaiah 7:14-15 predicts the virgin birth of Christ, 7:16 does not refer to him.[20] He thinks it 'regrettable' that English translations invariably suggest by their translation of *hanna'ar* ('the boy') that 7:16 speaks of the same child that is in 7:14-15. He translates 7:16: 'Before a boy knows enough to reject the wrong and choose the right, the land of the two kings you dread will be laid waste.' He recognizes that the Hebrew employs the article with the word 'boy,' but he cites *Gesenius' Hebrew Grammar*, 126q-r, to the effect that the Hebrew article may denote an indefinite person or thing that is present to the mind of the narrator, as grounds for his translation.

I acknowledge the validity of the syntactical rule he cites but question its applicability in this instance since in verse 14 specific reference is made to the virgin's 'son' (*bēn*) and in verse 15 *that* son is the antecedent referent of the third masculine singular form of the verb *yō'kēl* ('he will eat') and the third masculine singular suffix attached to the infinitive construct *ľdha'tō*, 'when he knows'). It is very unlikely, against this background, that *hanna'ar*, in the next verse (v. 16) would then refer to just any boy in general and not to the boy just mentioned. It is also striking, to say the least, that when precisely the same terms (*bēn...hanna'ar*) occur again only a few verses later (8:3-4), Vasholz himself translates: 'Before the boy [the 'son' referred to in the preceding verse] knows.'

---

[19]Payne, *Enyclopedia of Biblical Prophecy*, 291.

[20]Robert I. Vasholz, 'Isaiah and Ahaz: A Brief History of Crisis in Isaiah 7 and 8,' in *Presbyterion: Covenant Seminary Review* XIII/2 (Fall 1987):82-3.

4. Therefore, I believe that the solution proposed by J. Gresham Machen, E. J. Young, and R. Laird Harris is the best to date, all three arguing that the 'sign' is not to be restricted to the virgin's miraculous conception and to the unique character of her Son (7:14) but must include the words of 7:15-16 as well, and who, accordingly, make *the period of the early years of the miraculous child's life the measure of the time of Judah's dread*.[21]

In these two verses we are informed that the child would 'eat curds and honey when he knows enough to reject the wrong and choose the right.' What does this mean? According to Isaiah 7:21-22, 'curds and honey' would be the common fare of the remnant who remained in the land after the king of Assyria had assaulted the nation and deported much of its populace. Because of the diminished number of people in the land, there would be an abundance of milk, with the result that they 'will have curds to eat. All who remain in the land will eat curds and honey.' In other words, this aspect of God's sign to the House of David warned of a coming period of humiliation that, in light of verse 17, would envelop not only Israel but Judah as well *for a time*. The statement that the marvelous Immanuel Child would eat curds and honey symbolically meant then for Judah that the Immanuel child would identify himself with the remnant people from whom he would eventually come. But that the nation's then-present distress was to be a relatively short period of humiliation is evident from the fact that God declared that 'before the child knows enough to reject the wrong and choose the right, the land of the two kings you dread will be laid waste.' This time frame may be understood in either of two ways. It may mean that in the time it would take for the child to come to years of *moral* discretion, that is, within a period of a couple of years or so, the threat from the northern alliance would have been removed. If this is the intent of the 'time phrase,' God was saying that the time of dread for Judah would come to an end with the Assyrian invasion in 732 BC at which time Damascus fell and the northern kingdom was so despoiled (see 2 Kgs. 15:29) that for all intents and purposes it was only a 'rump' state during Hosea's reign. It could also be taken to mean that in the time it would take for the child to reach the age of *legal* accountability, that is, within a thirteen-year period (twelve years plus the original gestation period of the Child), the time of dread would come to an end. If this is the intent of the 'time phrase,' then God was referring to the period of time (if we commence the period from 734 BC) from 734 BC to 721 BC during which

---

[21] They differ only on details.

period of time both Damascus (in 732 BC) and Samaria (in 722 BC) were overthrown.

To sum up, then, it is not the time between the giving of the sign and its fulfillment that should be made the basis of relevance for Ahaz's day; rather, it is the time between the miraculous birth of the child and his coming to the age of discernment that makes the prophecy relevant to Ahaz's day.

Taking now the entire sign together, it is as if Isaiah had said, to employ Machen's paraphrase,

> I see a wonderful [virginally-conceived] child ... whose birth shall bring salvation to his people; and before such a period of time shall elapse as would lie between the conception of the child in his mother's womb and his coming to years of discretion [or legal accountability], the land of Israel and of Syria shall be forsaken.[22]

This paraphrase, endorsed in principle by both Young[23] and Harris,[24] takes all of the features of the sign into account and demonstrates how the sign, specifically because of the 'time' indicator attached to it, although not to be fulfilled for hundreds of years, nevertheless could have had – and did in fact have – relevance for Isaiah's contemporaries in that it provided them a measurable, relatively short time frame within which Judah's period of humiliation would come to an end.

As a parallel short-term prophetic sign that Judah's period of humiliation would be relatively short, God had Isaiah write on a large scroll the name, Maher-Shalal-Hash-Baz, which name – meaning as it does 'Quick to the plunder; swift to the spoil' – suggested an imminent assault from the Assyrians. He then had this act witnessed by two reliable witnesses. Then Isaiah 'went to the prophetess [doubtless his wife, and most likely at God's command], and she conceived and gave birth to a son.' God then commanded that the child should be named Maher-Shalal-Hash-Baz, and declared that before the boy would know how to say 'my father' or 'my mother,' Assyria would plunder Judah's two northern enemies (8:1-4). This

---

[22]J. Gresham Machen, *The Virgin Birth of Christ* (New York: Harper and Brothers, 1930), 293.

[23]Young, 'The Immanuel Prophecy,' in *Studies in Isaiah*, 190, 195-96.

[24]See R. Laird Harris's comment on Isaiah 7:14 in J. Oliver Buswell's *A Systematic Theology of the Christian Religion* (Grand Rapids: Zondervan, 1963), II, 548.

prophecy was surely fulfilled within the space of a year or so with Tiglath-pileser III's capture of Damascus and the spoilation of Samaria in 732 BC. And its fulfillment, in accordance with its stated short-term time feature, both confirmed and illustrated the similar time feature attached to the previous long-term Immanuel prophecy – enhancing thereby the latter's relevance to Isaiah's contemporaries.[25]

In my opinion, the interpretation of Isaiah 7:14-16 shared by Machen, Young, and Harris is to be preferred above all the others. I believe that they have demonstrated that the prophecy *exclusively* predicted Mary's virginal conception and the supernatural birth of Jesus Christ, and that in doing so it provided at the same time the time measure for the length of duration of Judah's eighth-century BC trouble as well. I would suggest also that Jesus' uniqueness as the uniquely conceived son of Mary came to expression precisely in terms of his being God incarnate, 'the Word become flesh,' as the name 'Immanuel' suggests.

Isaiah 9:6-7

When one considers the prophetic utterances in Isaiah 9:6-7 there can be no doubt that Isaiah of Jerusalem intended that we should recognize that we stand on messianic ground, as virtually all Old Testament scholars, even the most critical ones, will acknowledge. In his article on Isaiah 9:6, John D. Davis could list such scholars of his day as Briggs, Cheyne, Driver, G. A. Smith, Kirkpatrick, Skinner, Davidson, Dillmann, Kuenen, Guthe, Giesebrecht, Duhm, Cornill, Hackmann, Volz, Marti, Smend, and Nowack who admitted as much.[26] The list could certainly be extended today to include

---

[25]A variation on this explanation of the Isaiah 8 prophecy is that of J. A. Motyer in 'Context and Content in the Interpretation of Isaiah 7:14,' in *Tyndale Bulletin* 21 (1970):118-25, who, with the 'Machen-Young-Harris proposal,' understands the Immanuel prophecy to have single and direct fulfillment only in Christ but who also argues that Isaiah knew from the start that Judah and Jerusalem would ultimately fall, necessarily projecting the birth of Immanuel as the nation's ultimate hope into the undated future. Immanuel, in other words, was to inherit a 'disestablished' Davidic dynasty. Therefore, Isaiah 'introduced the second child into the sequence of prophecies (8:1-4), allowing Maher-Shalal-Hash-Baz *to take over from Immanuel* the task of providing a time-schedule for the immediately coming events' (124; emphasis supplied). But this proposal, it seems to me, 'disestablishes' the minority years of Immanuel from being the time indicator of a short period of devastation for Judah, the very thing which God himself declared that it was to be.

[26]See Davis's article, 'The Child Whose Name is Wonderful,' in *Biblical and Theological Studies* (New York: Charles Scribners, 1912), 93-108.

Davis himself, Alexander, Hengstenberg, Delitzsch, Mowinckel, Lindblom, Ringgren, Zimmerli, E. J.Young, J. Barton Payne, R. Laird Harris, Bruce K. Waltke, and Gleason L. Archer, Jr. In spite of the fact that some scholars, such as Gerhard von Rad, espouse the view that Isaiah – using ' high court language' on the order of that found in Egypt – speaks here of Hezekiah's ascension to Judah's throne,[27] nothing has been uncovered by modern Old Testament research that has convinced any evangelical scholar that he must abandon the traditional Christian interpretation which applies this prophecy to the Lord's Messiah.

Grammatical issues

That the two verbs in the perfect tense in 9:6a (*yulladh* and *nittan*; MT, 9:5a) are to be understood as prophetic perfects, that is, as verbs which describe the birth (and thus the reign) of this child as yet future to Isaiah, is evident from the entire context and also from the fact that no Davidic king prior to or during Isaiah's time, *including* Hezekiah, ever governed as Isaiah predicted that this king would do.This king, in fact, Isaiah prophesies, would realize in himself the consummation of the Davidic dynasty and reign forever. Isaiah writes:

> Of the increase of his government and peace there will be no end. He will reign on David's throne and over his kingdom, establishing and upholding it with justice and righteousness from that time on and forever (9:7).

These words are the prophetic soil from which later were to spring the words of the angel Gabriel who spoke to Mary of her future Child:

> He will be great and will be called the Son of the Most High. The Lord God will give him the throne of his father David, and he will reign over the house of Jacob forever; his kingdom will never end (Luke 1:32-33).

Surely Alexander's words, written over a century and a half ago, are as true today as they were when he wrote them:

> Upon the whole, it may be said with truth that there is no alleged prophecy of Christ, for which it seems so difficult with any plausibility to find another

---

[27]Gerhard von Rad, *Old Testament Theology* (New York: Harper & Row, 1965), II, 172.

subject; and until that is done, we may repose upon the old evangelical interpretation as undoubtedly the true one.[28]

I will approach this verse, then, standing on the well-founded assumption that it is directly and prophetically descriptive of the Messiah (who also fulfilled the earlier Immanuel prophecy of Isaiah 7:14), and proceed to a discussion of the significance of his names. The following is my translation of Isaiah 9:6:

> For a [male] child will be born to us,
> A son will be given to us.
> And one will call his name [that is, he shall be called]:
> Wonderful Counselor, Mighty God,
> Everlasting Father, Prince of Peace.

It is grammatically possible to construe the two nouns, *pele'* ('wonder[ful]') and *yo'ēts* ('counselor'), separately as two names, thus bringing the number of the Messiah's names here to five rather than four. But there are two decisive arguments in favor of taking the two nouns together as forming one name, first, the fact that the other three are compound titles, *'ēl gibbôr*, obviously a single title ('mighty God') as evidenced by its usage as a single designation for God in Isaiah 10:21 (see also Deut. 10:17; Ps. 24:8; Jer. 32:18; and Neh. 9:32), and the other two names being construct-absolute relationships ('Father of eternity,' 'Prince of peace'); and second, Isaiah's description of the Lord of Hosts as being 'wonderful in counsel' in Isaiah 28:29 where the same two roots are united to denote *one* characteristic in God.

As for the interpretation that makes the name 'Prince of peace' *alone* the Child's name, with 'wonderful Counselor, mighty God, eternal Father,' being construed as the compound subject of the verb 'will call,' it only needs to be said by way of rejoinder that in no other instance in the Hebrew Bible is the word 'name' separated by the subject of the sentence from the name itself.[29] And as for the suggestion of some that all of the titles are to be construed as one name and read as the sentence, 'The mighty God, the eternal Father, the Prince of peace is counseling a wonderful thing,' after noting that it has 'caused merriment among solemn commentators' – with

---

[28]J. A. Alexander, *The Earlier Prophecies of Isaiah* (New York: Wiley and Putnam, 1846), 167.

[29]Davis, 'The Child Whose Name is Wonderful,' in *Biblical and Theological Studies*, 96.

Dillman calling it an 'un-paralleled monstrosity' and Delitzsch speaking of it as a 'sesquipedalian name' – Davis notes the following objections to it: First, if the intention of the name is to emphasize the divine wisdom, why do the epithets of God not contribute to that object? Second, while it is true that 'Counselor' is in fact a participle (in the classical interpretation, the participle as a verbal adjective is construed nominally), since a verb is needed in the sentence, why is a participle employed rather than a perfect or imperfect verb form? Third, 'the title of "Prince of peace" belongs to the child and not to God according to the unmistakable context.'[30]

THE SETTING OF THE PROPHECY

The setting for this messianic prophecy is readily apparent from the context. Spiritual darkness blankets the land of Immanuel. Because God's chosen nation has resorted to sources other than the voice of God's prophets for spiritual guidance (8:19-20), the people 'roam through the land' in distress and gloom. But it will not always be so, declares the prophet Isaiah. It will come to pass that the spiritual darkness will be overcome. Suddenly, 'the people walking in darkness will see a great light; on those living in the land of the shadow of death a light will shine' (9:2; MT, 9:1). And where precisely does this 'great light' shine? In the regions of Zebulun and Naphtali (upper and lower Galilee), declares Isaiah (9:1; MT, 8:23), around the Sea of Galilee and the Jordan River, in the 'district of the nations' (or 'Galilee of the Gentiles') in which a large mixed population of Jews and Gentiles lived – a specific prediction, according to Matthew 4:13-16, of the Galilean portion of Jesus' ministry (see also John's references to Jesus as 'the Light' in the universal sense in John 1:4, 7-9; 8:12; 9:5). The effect of this sudden appearance of 'the great light' is two-fold (9:3; MT, 9:2): First, it enlarges the now-illumined nation (through the bringing in of the Gentiles) and, second, it replaces the people's previous gloom with joy (see Isa. 54:1; Luke 2:10; John 15:11; 16: 20-24; 17:13; Rom. 14:17; Gal. 5:22). Isaiah then gives three grounds in verses 4-7 (see the introductory *kî*, 'because') at vv. 4, 5, and 6; MT, vv. 3, 4, 5) for this new-found joy of the people: First, their deliverance from the bondage which had enslaved them; second, the destruction of all hostility (symbolized by the instruments of war) against them; and third and climactically, the birth of the Davidic King who will reign over them and through whom the previously-mentioned deliverance

---

[30]Davis, 'The Child Whose Name is Wonderful,' in *Biblical and Theological Studies*, 97.

and destruction were to be accomplished. There can be no doubt that Isaiah
intended this climactic third ground for rejoicing to be prophetic of the birth
and ministry of the Messiah, which prophecy the New Testament declares in
turn saw its fulfillment in the birth and ministry of Jesus Christ.

As a prophetic description of the Messiah, the opening couplet of this
climactic ground of rejoicing (9:6, MT, 9:5) is remarkable. The similarity
between Isaiah's 'a child *will be born to us*, … and the *government* will be' and
the angel's 'a Savior *has been born to you* … in the *city of David*' (Luke 2:11)
are, from a biblical-theological perspective, hardly accidental or incidental
– the one predicts and the other announces the fulfillment. The same can be
said for Isaiah's 'a son shall be given to us' (which means, when the passive
voice is rendered actively, 'God shall give a son to us') compared to the New
Testament phrase, 'God gave his Son' (John 3:16; Rom. 8:32; see John 4:10;
6:32). Neither can the similarity be accidental between this couplet together
with the phrase following it, namely, 'and one *will call his name…*' (which
means, 'and his name *will be called…*'), and Gabriel's later announcement:
'You will become pregnant and give birth to a son, and you will call his name
Jesus. He will be great and *will be called* the Son of the Most High … the
Power of the Most High will overshadow you; that is why [*dio kai*] the one to
be born *shall be called* holy. [After all, he is] the Son of God' (Luke 1:31-32,
35). According to Isaiah, this ruling child would be called by four exalted
names; and according to the angel Gabriel, this ruling child would be called
'Son of the Most High,' and 'Holy'. I am drawing attention to this parallel in
'name-calling' now, before we consider the names themselves in Isaiah 9:6,
to make the point that, though the phrase 'to call a name' is an idiom that can
in fact mean 'to name' in the sense of attaching an identifying proper noun
to someone as in the case of 'Jesus' (Matt. 1:21; Luke 1:31, but even here it
describes Jesus in his functional role as Savior), it may also intend that the
'name' one is given descriptively designates what one in fact is ontologically
(see Isa. 1:26; Hos. 1:10), as in the cases of 'Immanuel' in Matthew 1:23 and
(clearly from the context) 'Son of the Most High' and ' holy' in Luke 1:32,
35. It is in this latter sense, as with 'Immanuel' in Matthew 1:23 and 'Son of
the Most High' in Luke 1:32, that the four Isaianic names, I would submit,
are to be construed: not as names that the Child/Son would only bear
nominally (no child before or since Jesus was or has been so named), but
as names that *descriptively designate him as to his nature*, that is, names that
designate his characterizing attributes. Just as Mary's Son as 'Savior' was
named 'Jesus' but was in fact 'God with us,' 'Son of the Most High,' and

'holy', so here, I would suggest, we now learn that he is also in fact what these four marvelous names indicate. To discover what these names intend with respect to his character we will consider each name in turn.

'WONDERFUL COUNSELOR'

The translation, 'Wonderful Counselor,' is arrived at either (1) by construing 'wonder' (*pele'*) as standing in epexegetical construct to 'counselor' (*yoēts*), that is, 'a wonder of a counselor,' which means 'wonderful counselor', after the analogy of *kesîl 'ādhām* ('a fool of a man,' that is, 'a foolish man') in Proverbs 15:20, or (2) by construing ' wonder' independently as an absolute noun in apposition to 'counselor' ('a wonder [who is] a counselor,' that is, 'a counseling wonder'), after the analogy of *na'ᵃrāh bhᵉthûlāh*, 'a damsel [that is] a virgin,' that is, 'a virgin damsel') in Deuteronomy 22:23. The meaning is virtually the same in either case: 'As a counselor, he is a wonder,' which is just to say that the Child/Son is a 'wonderful counselor'.

As for its meaning, we must not ascribe to the word 'wonder' its modern debased denotation which permits it to be attached to the most mundane of things ('I had a wonderful time in the country,' 'You have a wonderful class schedule,' etc.). The significant feature about this first title is that the word for 'wonder' (*pele'*) and the *niphal* participial form from the same root (the root meaning of both being 'separation', and hence remoteness, inaccessibility, and impossibility) is always employed only in relationship to God (the occurrence in Lam. 1:9 is not really an exception when one recalls that it was God who effected the 'wonder' of Jerusalem's destruction before both Israel and the surrounding nations) to denote his wondrous miracles in behalf of the salvation of his people and his horrible judgments against his enemies (Exod. 3:20; 15:11; 34:10; Josh. 3:5; Neh. 9:17; 1 Chron. 16:12; Pss. 40:5 (MT, v. 6); 77:11 (MT, v. 12), 14 (MT, v. 15); 78:12; 136:4; 139:14; Isa. 25:1). Particularly instructive for our present purpose is its occurrence in Judges 13:18 when in response to Manoah's request for his name, the Angel of the Lord replied: 'It is *peli'y*' (that is, 'wonderful,' or 'beyond human comprehension'), following his announcement by doing the 'wonderful thing' (*maphli'*, v. 19) of ascending in the flame of Manoah's sacrifice (13:20). Then when we read in Isaiah 28:29 that the Lord of Hosts is 'wonderful in counsel and magnificent in wisdom,' literally, that the Lord of Hosts 'caused [his] counsel to be wonderful and [his] wisdom to be magnificent,' we must conclude that when the Child/Son of Isaiah 9:6 is named 'wonderful counselor,' this title is ascribing an attribute characteristic of the Lord of Hosts himself to the one so named, indicating thereby his divine wisdom and by extension his deity. In the execution of his prerogatives as Davidic ruler, the Child/Son will govern with wisdom that is nothing short of just the wisdom of God himself for he is himself divine.

'MIGHTY GOD'

The Messiah's second name, 'Mighty God,' *'ēl gibbôr*,[31] is arrived at by construing *gibbôr* ('mighty') adjectivally with *'ēl* ('God') after the analogy of *shaddai*, in the joint name of *'ēl shaddai* ('Almighty God') in Genesis 17:1. All of the efforts through such translations as 'a God-like hero' (Kautzsch) or 'a mighty hero' (Gesenius) to reduce the title in meaning to something less than deity, as Delitzsch says, 'founder, without needing any further refutation,' on the recurring instances of this title as a designation of God himself in Deuteronomy 10:17, Psalm 24:8, Jeremiah 32:18, Nehemiah 9:32, and especially Isaiah 10:21 where it is used beyond all question of God himself.[32] There can be no doubt that its meaning is 'mighty God.'

But are we to understand this title as a description of the nature of the Messiah? In response to this question, it is important to note that in Psalm 45:6 (MT, 45:7) the Messiah is addressed as 'God' (*'elōhîm*) in the fullest sense of the word (see Heb. 1:8). We may also take note of the additional fact that earlier in the same Psalm (v. 3; MT, v. 4), the Messiah is addressed as 'mighty one' (*gibbôr*). Thus we see that there is willingness on the part of the Old Testament witness elsewhere to address the Messiah by both terms in the same context. Isaiah is hardly setting a precedent then when he utilizes a title for God in which the two terms have been brought together as an epithet of the divine Messiah. And if, as the Author of Hebrews affirms (1:8), the intention of Psalm 45 is to ascribe nothing less than unabridged deity to the Messiah, then there is nothing except dogmatic prejudice which prohibits the conclusion that Isaiah intended to do the same thing here. Since this is what Isaiah 7:14 intends as well by its description of the Messiah as Immanuel ('God [is] with us'), I would submit that the second title in Isaiah 9:6 intends to predicate of the Child/Son just deity itself and specifically the divine might

---

[31]See Benjamin B. Warfield, 'The Divine Messiah in the Old Testament,' in *Biblical And Theological Studies* (Philadelphia: Presbyterian and Reformed, 1952), 104-16, for his trenchant analysis of the critical handling of this name by the leading Old Testament scholars of his day.

[32]Franz Delitzsch, *Biblical Commentary on the Prophecies of Isaiah*, translated by James Martin (Third German edition; Grand Rapids: Eerdmans, 1877), I, 252.

of the Deity. And in this context this means that the Messiah, as he governs with divine wisdom (see 'wonderful Counselor') exercises the attribute of divine might as well. His first two names then describe what the Messiah is in himself, with the former describing his wisdom to counsel (govern) and the latter his power to execute it.

'EVERLASTING FATHER'

Because of the construct-absolute relationship between the two nouns in the third name *'abhi 'adh*, and because the noun *'adh*, means here 'perpetuity' as it does in the genitive connection in Isaiah 45:17 (see 57:15), there can be no doubt that the phrase is to be translated 'Everlasting Father,' after the analogy of *har kodhshî*, literally, 'the hill of my holiness,' that is, 'my holy hill') in Psalm 2:6.[33] The efforts by some scholars, through such translations as 'father of booty', to rid the title of the implication of unendingness shatter on the phrases surrounding it in the context: 'Of the increase of his government and peace there will be no end' and 'He will reign … from that time on and forever' (9:7; MT, 9:6). At the very least, this title suggests that the Messiah in some sense is possessed of no mere mortality. And this perception is strengthened by the fact that the passage itself teaches that he, as the realization in himself of the culmination of the Davidic line with no succession of rulers after him, will reign over his kingdom as long as the latter endures, which is just to say, forever.

The Christian mind must be careful here not to confuse the Son with God the Father because the Son is designated here as a 'father'. The prophet had already made it clear that the Messiah is God's son ('a son shall be given'). What then does the word 'father' as a characterization of the Messiah mean here? This name, as with the other two, must be restricted to its contextual universe as a description in some sense of the 'given Son', which is just to say that the title affirms that as the Messiah rules with divine wisdom and power from David's throne, his rule – notwithstanding his might – will be *paternal in character*. He will view his subjects as his *children* and will, as a result, wield his scepter for their benefit. Citing Gesenius, Delitzsch, Dillmann, Cheyne, Skinner and Marti, Davis writes.

It is exegetically needful … to give to the word ['adh] in the messianic title its customary sense of endurance, continuance, and render the title 'father

---

[33]Gesenius' *Hebrew Grammar*, 440, par. 135n; see also 417, par. 128p.

of endurance' and understand the designation to denote *a continual father, one who enduringly acts as a father to his people.*[34]

This paternal 'father to child' relationship is precisely that which the Author of Hebrews declares governed the Son in his willingness (as their messianic king and priest after the order of Melchizedek) to share in the humanity of his 'children' (Heb. 2:13-14). And it is precisely this caring paternity that we see the incarnate Son exercising already toward the paralytic in Mark 2:5 and Matthew 9:2 when he addresses him as 'child' (*teknon*) and toward the sick woman in Mark 5:34 whom he addresses as his 'daughter' (*thugatēr*). In this third name, then, we see yet another divine quality – the quality of mercy – ascribed to the Messiah as he enduringly acts as a father toward his people.

'PRINCE OF PEACE'
The fourth name *sar shālôm* ('prince of peace'), like the third a construct-absolute construction in the Hebrew, adds nothing to the Messiah's character insofar as his deity is concerned. It does, however, provide insight into his kingly office, suggesting that the Messiah by his reign will institute, promote, and maintain peace (see Isa. 2:4; 9:6; 11:6-9; Micah 4:3-4; 5:4-5a; Hos. 2:18). And to the degree that this particular work of the Messiah is divine work alone, just to that same degree his own divine character is reflected in the specialized work that he does. All the more is this evident when it is recalled, first, that Messiah's 'peace work' necessarily involves the cessation of all earthly warfare and the destruction of the cause of all this warfare – human sin (Jam. 4:1-2), and second, that he extends this work *universally* (see the phrases, 'Of the increase of his government and peace there will be no end [geographically]', and, 'from now on and forever [to the farthest reaches of the future]').

Such 'peace work' in turn certainly means that God and man must be reconciled. But can anyone legitimately doubt that only the Messiah in the person of Jesus Christ, through whom alone, according to Scripture, men may find peace with God (Rom. 5:1), who himself

is our peace, who made both [Jews and Gentiles] one and destroyed the enmity, the regulations, in order that he might create in himself one new

[34]Davis, 'The Child Whose Name is Wonderful,' in *Biblical and Theological Studies*, 105 (emphasis supplied).

THE LAMB DEIFIED: ISAIAH 7:14-16; 9:6-7

man out of the two, *thus making peace*, and [in order] that he might *reconcile both in one body to God* through the cross, slaying the enmity [of God] by it. And having come he preached the good news of peace to you who were far off and of peace to those who were near (Eph. 2:14-17) –

can anyone legitimately doubt, I ask, that Scripture would have us believe that Jesus Christ is Isaiah's 'Prince of Peace' and that he alone completely fulfills the role implied in this fourth great name? And surely in doing so, he floods the name with all the divine glory and power of his own essential being!

We have seen that Isaiah confronts us with the divine 'Child of the Four Exalted Titles' – 'Wonderful Counselor, Mighty God, Everlasting Father, Prince of Peace.' As a summary of this great messianic passage, I cannot improve upon Delitzsch's insight – for surely he is right – when he declares:

> …the words [of Isa. 9:6] in their strict meaning point to the Messiah, whom men may for a time, with pardonable error, have hoped to find in Hezekiah, but whom, with unpardonable error, men refused to acknowledge, even when He actually appeared in Jesus. The name Jesus is the combination of all the Old Testament titles used to designate the Coming One according to his nature and his works. The names contained in ch. vii. 14 and ix. 6 are not thereby suppressed; but they have continued, from the time of Mary downwards, in the mouth of all believers. There is not one of these names under which worship and homage have not been paid to Him. But we never find them crowded together anywhere else, as we do here in Isaiah; and in this respect also our prophet proves himself the greatest of the Old Testament evangelists.[35]

And for our present purpose all this means that the messianic Lamb of God would be God in the unabridged sense of that word.

---

[35]Delitzsch, *Biblical Commentary on the Prophecies of Isaiah*, 251.

67

CHAPTER EIGHT

THE LAMB PERSONIFIED:
ISAIAH 52:13–53:12

Isaiah 52:13–53:12, the so-called 'Fourth Servant Song' of Isaiah, depicts
the Servant of the Lord as a *suffering* Servant under the figure of a *person*
'led like a lamb [*seh*; LXX, probaton] to the slaughter, and as a sheep [*rāchēl*;
LXX, *amnos*] before her shearers is silent, so he did not open his mouth'
(53:7). Johannes Gess writes: 'Here [in Isa. 53:7] for the first time a person
is spoken of as fulfilling the function of a sacrificial animal.'[1]

It is striking that in the two passages in the Old Testament where Israel's
future Deliverer actually receives three times the title of 'Messiah', there is
the strong intimation that his ministry will entail not only a regal but also a
tragic dimension. In Psalm 2:2, read in the light of verse 7 which speaks of
his resurrection from the dead (see Acts 13:33), the Lord's 'Anointed One'
is confronted with united hostility from Jew and Gentile which apparently
eventuates in his death. And in Daniel 9:25-26, we are informed: 'Messiah
will be cut off and will have nothing [or, '...cut off but not for himself']'.

This tragic dimension in Messiah's work is both poignantly and
powerfully displayed in Isaiah's 'Fourth Servant Song,' foretelling that the
Messiah would as God's Lamb suffer unto death for sinners. We may outline
this Song as follows:

Introduction: The enigma of the Lord's servant (52:13-15)
  I.   His infancy and youth (53:1-2)
  II. His maturity (53:3)

---

[1]Johannes Gess, 'Lamb,' in *The New International Dictionary of New Testament Theology*,
edited by Colin Brown (Grand Rapids: Zondervan, 1976), 2:410.

III. His sufferings (53:4-6)

IV. His trial and death (53:7-8)

V. His burial (53:9)

VI. His resurrection and vindication (53:10)

VII. The fruit of his labors (53:11-12)

Conclusion: Alternative responses to the Lord's servant (52:15b and 53:1)

THE LITERARY SETTING OF THIS SONG

In Isaiah 41–53 are found what most scholars, following Bernhard Duhm's 1892 commentary on Isaiah,[2] designate as the four 'Servant Songs'. The first is found in 42:1-4, the second in 49:1-6, the third in 50:4-9, and the fourth in 52:13–53:12. The principle underlying this specific selection of Songs is that all four portray a single distinctive figure. Because the limits of these songs are not always clear, some scholars have added verses 5-7 to the first, verse 7 to the second, and verses 10 and 11 to the third, and some, O.T. Allis,[3] for instance, even regard Isaiah 61:1-3 as a fifth Servant Song.

Because the nation of Israel is addressed in the second song (49:3) as 'my [God's] servant,' some scholars read a *corporate* notion into the 'servant' in *all* these songs. As we will see, this cannot be made to work exegetically. Other scholars, while acknowledging that the 'servant' refers to an *individual*, suggest that that individual is either some unknown contemporary of Isaiah or the so-called 'Deutero-Isaiah' or a known individual such as Cyrus, Jeremiah, Zerubbabel, or Isaiah himself. This view, we will see shortly, cannot be made to work exegetically either. The most satisfying view, I maintain, is the *three-dimensional* view put forward by Franz Delitzsch[4] using the figure of a pyramid, in which (1) Israel, as the base of the pyramid, in some contexts is God's servant who is charged with the twofold responsibility of bearing witness to the true God before the heathen nations and serving as the custodian of his revealed and inscripturated Word (Isa. 41:8-9, 42:18-19, 44:1, 44:21, 45:4, 48:20, 49:3 [within the second song]); (2) in one context (43:10), as the central section of the pyramid, the elect remnant in Israel ('Israel not only of the flesh but also of the spirit') is God's servant charged

---

[2]Bernhard Duhm, *Das Buch Jesaia* (Fifth edition; Göttingen, 1892).

[3]O. T. Allis, *The Unity of Isaiah* (Philadelphia: Presbyterian and Reformed, 1950), 82.

[4]Franz Delitzsch, *Biblical Commentary on the Prophecies of Isaiah* (Reproduction of the 1877 translation by James Martin; Grand Rapids: Eerdmans, n. d.), II, 174.

with the responsibility of bearing witness to God's character before their unspiritual countrymen; and (3) in the four contexts mentioned above, as the apex of the pyramid, the Messiah himself is God's Servant.

If we are right about this three-dimensional division of the Servant material in Isaiah, then interestingly, in the first of the songs about him, the Messiah is set forth as one who has the task of establishing justice in the earth and who will complete that mission successfully. In the second are intimations that he will be confronted with opposition in the execution of his mission of restoring Israel to God's favor (see 'I have labored to no purpose; I have spent my strength in vain and for nothing,' 49:4). In the third the Messiah himself speaks about the personal suffering that he will face but he gives no reasons for his suffering (see 'I offered my back to those who beat me ... I did not hide my face from mocking and from spitting,' 50:6). Accordingly, it is reserved for the fourth climactic Servant Song to inform us why the Servant must suffer: he must bear the sin of many! This then is the literary setting of the Song.

THE CORPORATE INTERPRETATION OF THIS SONG

As we have noted, many scholars want us to believe that the Servant of Yahweh in this Song is to be viewed corporately as the nation of Israel. Can this view be sustained? A careful reading of the Song by the unbiased student will show

1. that the servant is
   a. portrayed as divine ('the arm of the Lord,' 53:1[5]);
   b. portrayed in detailed features as a *human personality* (52:14; 53:2-3);
   c. portrayed as an innocent, indeed, sinless sufferer (53:4, 5, 8d, 9c-d, 12d);
   d. portrayed as a voluntary sufferer (53:7a);
   e. portrayed as an obedient, humble, and silent sufferer (53:7); and

2. that his suffering
   a. springs from his love for sinners, including his executioners who act in ignorance (53:4c-d, 7, 12);

---

[5]See J. Alec Motyer, *The Prophecy of Isaiah: An Introduction and Commentary* (InterVarsity, 1993), 427, for the exegetical argument.

b. is ordained by God in love and fulfills the divine will and purpose (53:10);

c. deals with sin in all its aspects (see the word 'sin,' that is, specific acts of missing the mark, 53:12; 'transgressions,' that is, willful acts of rebellion, 53:5; 'iniquities,' that is, moral evil, 53:5);

d. is vicarious, that is, substitutionary (53:4a-b, 5a-b, 6c, 8-9d, 10b, 11d, 12e);

e. is redemptive and spiritual in nature (53:5c-d, 11d);

f. ends in his death (53:8a, c-d, 10a, 12c) which leads to his being buried with the rich (53:9-10), which condition gives way to his resurrection (53:10b-d, 11);

g. leads the straying people for whom he died to confession and repentance (53:4-6); and finally,

h. as his redemptive work, in implementing a divine plan in which suffering, humiliation, and death are central, inaugurates a fruitful and victorious life for endless ages (53:10c-d, 11a-b, 12a-b).[6]

Can these personal characteristics of the Servant's suffering designate the nation of Israel viewed historically, spiritually, or ideally? I am compelled to answer in the negative for the following reasons:

1. Scripture knows no parallel case where, without any hint of allegory, a passage maintains a personification of Israel throughout the entire section with no indication of its meaning.

2. The words in Isaiah 53:8, '...for the transgression of my people [pesha' 'ammî] he was stricken,' makes the application of the passage to Israel as the Servant untenable since the prophet's 'people' are clearly Israel, but if the servant is Israel how can Israel be slain for Israel?

3. Israel as a nation has never been an innocent sufferer. In Isaiah 1:4 the prophet speaks of Israel as a 'sinful nation, a people loaded with guilt, a brood of evildoers, children given to corruption,' and in the nearer context of 42:23-25 he states that Israel's affliction is God's judgment upon the nation for its sins.

---

[6]I have adapted these points from Frederick Alfred Aston, *The Challenge of the Ages* (Scarsdale: New York: Research, 1968), 8.

4. Israel as a nation has never been a voluntary sufferer. Never did the nation voluntarily go into exile; each exile was the result of a humiliating national defeat.

5. Israel as a nation has never been an obedient, humble, and silent sufferer. No sooner was the nation delivered from Egypt than it rebelled and complained against the privations of the wilderness. Even such great biblical personalities as Job, Moses, David, Elijah, and Jeremiah complained bitterly about their lot at times.

6. Israel as a nation never endured suffering out of love for others. Since the nation's suffering was neither innocent nor voluntary nor silent, it cannot be said that its suffering was motivated by love for others.

7. Israel as a nation never suffered because God out of love for the nation divinely ordained that it would *innocently* suffer. Israel's suffering is always portrayed as the consequence of her transgressions (Deut. 28:62-68; Isa. 40:2b; 42:23-25).

8. Israel as a nation never suffered vicariously for other nations. Yet throughout this passage the idea of vicarious suffering providing atonement for others occupies the most prominent place, being expressed no less than 23 times in 9 of the 15 verses.

9. Israel's suffering as a nation *per se* has not brought redemption to the world. Nowhere does Scripture teach that Israel will be redeemed by its own suffering, far less that it can or will redeem other nations or that *its* suffering will redeem the nations of mankind from the power of sin. Since Israel's suffering as a nation has been neither innocent nor voluntary nor silent, it can have no intrinsic moral value and no redemptive power.

10. Israel's suffering as a nation has not ended in its demise, either historically or ideally, while every ancient nation that existed in the Old Testament contemporaneously with Israel has long since passed into oblivion.

11. Israel's suffering as a nation has not brought about its experiencing moral or spiritual resurrection, either historically or ideally. Since there was no national death there cannot be and there has been no national resurrection. And spiritually speaking, the nation remains by and large in unbelief to this day.

12. Israel's suffering as a nation has neither produced a moral transformation of the nations nor caused them to come to Israel's

God with the penitence and confession of guilt which occupies the prominent place that it does in this passage.

13. Israel's suffering as a nation has never resulted in the nation's glorification. No restoration of Israel from exile lifted the nation from extreme humiliation to sublime exaltation.

If Israel's suffering as a nation has in the past and will in the future bring great redemptive blessing to the other nations of the world, one must wonder why the synagogue readings from the prophets always omit this 'Fourth Servant Song' while the portions immediately preceding and following it are read?

Moreover, if the leaders of world Jewry really believe that this chapter depicts the nation of Israel by its suffering atoning for the nations, why do they not read it in public? What could be more comforting in a memorial service for Jews who perished in the gas chambers of Treblinka and Auschwitz or who struggled to survive in the Warsaw ghetto than the divine promise: 'My [suffering] servant justifies many and bears their guilt' (53:11)? To the thousands who mourn relatives killed in the Nazi fury what could be more consoling than the assurance that their loved ones' deaths were not in vain but were in fact the climactic aspect of God's grand plan for the redemption of the nations?[7] As the situation stands now, however, unless it changes, I believe that someday world Jewry will rise up and condemn its rabbinic and synagogical leadership for refusing to acquaint the Jewish people with Isaiah's marvelous predictive prophecy of their Messiah who would lay down his life for the sin of others and rise from the dead for their justification.

In sum, I must conclude that the corporate view does not fit and cannot be made to fit the terms of the Song exegetically. One could even conclude with some justification that the corporate view is put forward primarily to avoid the prophet's obvious design – that the passage depicts, and is intended to depict, a specific person.

THE PERSONAL INTERPRETATION OF THIS SONG

Among the voices who contend that the Song speaks of a specific individual – a fact not generally known – is that of the Ancient Synagogue that taught that the prophet is speaking here of an individual of transcendent influence who ranks morally and spiritually above any and every other character of the Old Testament, and therefore it applied the passage to the Messiah.[8] In

---

[7] I have adapted these points from Aston, *The Challenge of the Ages*, 8-14.

fact, according to R. T. France, 'the evidence … suggests that in Palestinian Judaism of the time of Christ and afterward a messianic exegesis of the Servant was so firmly established that even the demands of the anti-Christian polemic could not unseat it.'[9] Later, such rabbis as Rabbi Naphtali Ben Asher Altschuler and Rabbi Mosheh Alsheh in the late sixteenth/early seventeen centuries also applied this Song specifically to the Messiah.

THE MESSIANIC REFERENT OF THIS SONG

There are scholars, however, who argue that the individual is simply a martyr, perhaps Isaiah himself or perhaps Jeremiah. But an insuperable burden rests upon these scholars to make the case that the martyrdom of Isaiah, 'Deutero-Isaiah,'[10] Jeremiah or some other Israelite saint[11] meets the demands of a fair reading of the Song. After all, they were all sinners who would need redemption themselves. Indeed, Isaiah himself declares: 'All we [this 'all' would necessarily include Isaiah, Jeremiah, and any other Old Testament saint] like sheep have gone astray; we have turned every one to his own way' (53:6). Moreover, to assert that the martyrdom of even the most pious forgiven saint would or ever could bring about the redemption of the world is entirely foreign to the entire Old Testament where one will search in vain for a eulogy of even the greatest of Israel's heroes save one, that is, the Messiah.

Who then is the Servant, if not some Old Testament saint? Find such a person as this Song describes and one finds the Servant/Messiah. All the difficulties that the other views entail disappear when the passage is applied personally to Jesus of Nazareth, for he (and, we may say parenthetically, he

---

[8]See Aston, *The Challenge of the Ages*, 14-17, who cites the *Targum Yonathan ben Uzziel*, the *Midrash Cohen*, the *Midrash Rabbah* of Rabbi Mosheh Haddarsham, and the Musaph service of the Day of Atonement to this effect.

[9]R. T. France, 'Servant of the Lord,' in *The Zondervan Pictorial Encyclopedia of the Bible*, edited by Merrill C. Tenney (Grand Rapids: Zondervan, 1975), 5.361.

[10]The mere fact that the verb tenses of much of the Fourth Song are perfects means nothing. The 'prophetic perfect' is a recognized use of the perfect aspect of the verb. On this point, see O. Palmer Robertson, *The Christ of the Prophets* (Phillipsburg, N. J.: Presbyterian and Reformed, 2004), 480. Moreover, just as the Cyrus prophecy in Isaiah 44:24-28 places Cyrus in the distant future from Isaiah's perspective (see O. T. Allis, *The Unity of Isaiah*, chapters 5–7), so also the Fourth Song places the suffering Servant in the distant future from Isaiah's perspective.

[11]According to O. T. Allis in his *The Unity of Isaiah*, 90, during his own professional career some fifteen different individuals who figured more or less prominently in Old Testament history had been suggested as the servant intended by the Fourth Song.

alone[12]) meets all the demands of the details of this magnificent prophetic Song. This assertion is clearly substantiated by the following New Testament data:

1. Jesus was both a historical human person, born in lowliness (Matt. 2:1; Luke 2:1-2), and divine (Rom. 9:5; Titus 2:13; Heb. 1:8; 2 Pet. 1:1; John 1:1, 18; 20:28; 1 John 5:20).
2. He was an innocent person (John 8:46).
3. He was despised and rejected by men and was unjustly executed as a felon (Luke 23:13-15).
4. He was a voluntary sufferer (John 10:17-18; Gal. 2:20).
5. He was an obedient, humble, and silent sufferer (Matt. 27:12, 14; Phil. 2:8; 1 Pet. 2:23).
6. He suffered out of love for others (Luke 23:34).
7. He suffered in order to fulfill the divine plan and will (Eph. 3:11).
8. He suffered vicariously for his people (1 Pet. 2:24).
9. He suffered in order to provide a redemptive intervention in the course of history leading to the justification of the evildoer from his sin (1 Cor. 1:30; 1 Pet. 1:18-19).
10. He suffered to the point of death (Matt. 27:50).
11. His death gave way to the resurrection (1 Cor. 15:4).
12. He ascended, after his resurrection from the dead, to heaven and is now highly exalted, sitting on the right hand of God (Phil. 2:9-11).[13]

All of these features of Jesus' life comport beautifully with the demanding details of the fourth Servant Song. Can anyone validly write any other name under the Song's amazing verbal portrait than the name of Jesus of Nazareth? Beyond all controversy, the New Testament regards him as the Song's referent.

NEW TESTAMENT TEACHING ABOUT THE SONG'S REFERENT

John the Baptist, by his use of the descriptive phrase with reference to Jesus, 'the Lamb of God who takes away the sin of the world' (John 1:29, 36), seems to have been drawing from Isaiah's Fourth Servant Song when he said

---

[12]One must decide whether Jesus alone bore the sins of his people or whether someone other than he could do and in fact did this. For myself, only Jesus could and did die for my sins.

[13]I have adapted these points from Aston, *The Challenge of the Ages*, 18.

this. Morna D. Hooker may believe that there is 'no convincing evidence to suggest that Isaiah 53 played any significant role in Jesus' own understanding of his ministry',[14] but Jesus self-consciously applied the role of the sacrificial Servant of Isaiah 53 to himself and taught others to believe that he was the Servant spoken of here. For example, he expressly applied the vicarious death of Isaiah's suffering Servant to himself in Luke 22:37: 'This Scripture [referring to Isaiah 53:12],' he declared, 'must be fulfilled *in me*. Yes, what is written about me is reaching its fulfill-ment.' After his resurrection the risen Christ said to his perplexed disciples on the road to Emmaus: 'How foolish you are, and how slow of heart to believe all that the prophets have spoken! Did not the Messiah have to suffer these things [I just suffered] and then enter his glory?' Luke then declares: 'And beginning with Moses and all the Prophets [which surely would have included this Song], [Jesus] *explained* to them what was said in all the Scriptures *concerning himself*' (24:25-27). That Luke intended by his phrase, 'all the Scriptures,' specifically the Scriptures of the Old Testament is clear from the words of Jesus that he cites a few verses later: 'Everything must be fulfilled that has been written *about me* in the Law of Moses and the Prophets and the Psalms' (Luke 24:44).[15] 'Then,' Luke recounts, 'he opened [his disciples'] minds so they could understand *the Scriptures*.' He told them, '*This is what is written*: The Messiah will suffer and rise from the dead on the third day, and repentance and forgiveness of sins will be preached in his name to all nations, beginning at Jerusalem' (Luke 24:45-47).

Students of the four Gospels have detected other references to Isaiah 53 even in single words and phrases in the sayings of Jesus, for example, his use of the word 'rejected' in Mark 9:12 (see Isa. 53:3), and his expression 'taken away' in Mark 2:20 (see Isa. 53:8). Furthermore, Isaiah 53:7 seems to be reflected in Jesus' deliberate silence before his judges (see Mark 14:61; 15:5; Luke 23:9; John 19:9), Isaiah 53:12 in his intercession for his executioners

---

[14]Morna D. Hooker, 'Did the Use of Isaiah 53 to Interpret His Mission Begin with Jesus?' in *Jesus and the Suffering Servant: Isaiah 53 and Christian Origins*, edited by William H. Bellinger, Jr. and William R. Farmer (Harrisburg, PA: Trinity Press International, 1998), 88.

[15]Jesus' description of the Old Testament here as 'the Law of Moses and the Prophets and the Psalms' probably reflects the tripartite division of the Old Testament canon (tôrâh, nᵉbhî'îm, kᵉthûbhîm) that clearly already existed in some form in the second century BC. See Edward J. Young, *An Introduction to the Old Testament* (Grand Rapids: Eerdmans, 1960), 32, and Gleason L. Archer, Jr., *A Survey of Old Testament Introduction*, 79.

(see Luke 23:34), and Isaiah 53:10 in his 'laying down his life' for others (see John 10:11, 15, 17). Martin Hengel, in fact, has argued that Isaiah 53 as a whole provides the basis for both Jesus' famous 'ransom sayings' (Matt. 20:28; Mark 10:45) and his 'supper sayings' (Matt. 26:26-28; Mark 14:22-24).[16] R. T. France does not appear to be amiss then when he states that all the Evangelists 'accepted [the figure of the Servant of Yahweh] as an appropriate and illuminating model for Jesus' mission of vicarious suffering and death for the sins of his people.'[17]

His disciples clearly grasped from his teaching the connection that Jesus specifically drew between Isaiah 53 as prophecy and himself as its *personal* fulfillment, for we find the following things recorded in the New Testament about this Song:

1. Philip, when asked by the Ethiopian eunuch about whom Isaiah spoke in 53:7-8, 'beginning with this scripture, told him about Jesus' (Acts 8:30-35);
2. Paul refers to Isaiah 53:12 in Philippians 2:7;[18]
3. Peter alludes to Isaiah 53:5, 6, 9, and 11 in 1 Peter 2:22-25; 3:18;
4. Matthew refers Isaiah 53:4 to Jesus in Matthew 8:17;
5. the Author of Hebrews in 7:27, 9:12, 25-26, 28; 10:10-14 alludes to Isaiah 53:4-6 when he declares that Christ was offered once for all times to bear the sins of many; and
6. John uses Isaiah 53:1 in John 12:38.

In light of both the predictive character of Isaiah's Fourth Servant Song and these explicit usages of Isaiah 53 by Jesus and the New Testament writers, the

---

[16]Martin Hengel, *The Atonement: The Origin of the Doctrine in the New Testament*, translated by John Bowden (London: SCM, 1981), 33-75.

[17]R. T. France, 'Servant of Yahweh,' in *Dictionary of Jesus and the Gospels*, edited by Joel B. Green, Scot McKnight, and I. Howard Marshall (Downers Grove, Illinois: InterVarsity, 1992), 746a.

[18]See my exegesis of Philippians 2:7 in *A New Systematic Theology of the Christian Faith* (Nashville, Tenn.: Thomas Nelson, 1998), 263, where I have argued that the Pauline phrase 'himself he emptied' is the dynamic equivalent to Isaiah's expression in 53:12, 'He poured himself out unto death.' The so-called 'kenosis' phrase in this pericope has for its background then our Lord's high-priestly ministry and refers to the Messiah's Lamb work for sinners and not to a 'self-emptying' on his part of some of his divine attributes alleged by some to have occurred in the act of the Incarnation.

church from the beginning to the present has believed itself to be justified in seeing both adumbrations and explicit descriptions of the cross work of Jesus Christ throughout Isaiah 53. Therefore, we must not hesitate to call the world's attention to this passage and to teach about Jesus and his Lamb work from it.

CHAPTER NINE

THE LAMB IDENTIFIED:
JOHN 1:29, 35

When we turn to the pages of the New Testament we find, according to the
testimonies of Gabriel, Zechariah, Jesus himself, the Synoptic Evangelists,
and the Fourth Evangelist, that John the Baptist was the Elijah of Malachi 4:5
who was to go before the Lord to prepare the way before him (Mal. 3:1).
And what a mighty work of preparation he did! By identifying Jesus Christ
in six ways John pointed with unimpeachable clarity to him as the one whose
way it was his task to prepare (Matt. 3:11-13; Mark 1:7; Luke 3:16-17;
John 1:15, 26, 29-35; 3:26-36; see John 1:6-9, 5:35; Acts 19:4).

JOHN'S IDENTIFYING WITNESS: JESUS IS THE SPIRIT BAPTIZER (MATT. 3:10-12;
MARK 1:7-8; LUKE 3:16-17)
Prior to his baptism of Jesus, John had announced to the people coming to
him: 'I am baptizing you with water unto repentance. But he who comes
after me is mightier than I, whose sandals I am not worthy to carry. He
shall baptize you with the Holy Spirit and [judge you] with fire.' In this
declaration John states that the Coming One was possessed of a lofty,
exalted, kingly office. But his words intend far more, for he says that this
one's prerogatives included the granting of *eternal salvation* ('he will baptize
with the Holy Spirit') and the executing of *eternal judgment* ('and [judge]
with fire' – see the parallelism in the three occurrences of 'fire' at the end
of verses 10, 11, 12, the occurrences of 'fire' in Luke 3:16-17, and the fact
that where Mark does not mention the '[judging] with fire,' neither does he
mention any other reference to fire). This, by the way, explains the reason
for the Baptist's insistence in his intercourse with Jesus later that he had need
of being baptized (with salvation) by Jesus (Matt. 3:14). Such prerogatives

belong only to one with divine stature (see the parallelism between the two 'this is…' statements in John 1:33 and 1:34); only God can exercise such authority!

JOHN'S IDENTIFYING WITNESS: JESUS, THE ONE 'AFTER' JOHN, IS THE YAHWEH OF THE OLD TESTAMENT (JOHN 1:15, 30)

When John was asked about his relation to the one coming after him, twice he expressed himself in the following words:

> He who comes *after* me [or, 'One is coming after me who'] *was before me* [*emprosthen mou gegonen*], because [*hoti*] he *was before me* [*prōtos mou ēn*].

Here is a magnificent statement on John's part. BAGD suggests that the middle assertion (*emprosthen mou gegonen*) has to do with status and they translate the phrase accordingly: 'ranks higher than I.'[1] But there are sound reasons for moving in a different direction from evidence that suggests that John is thinking *temporally*, that is, in terms of time, throughout the verse. This is certainly his intent in the first clause ('He who comes *after* me') and almost as certainly his intent in the third clause ('he *was* [*ēn*] before me,' the *ēn* here doubtless having as its background the three occurrences of *ēn* in John 1:1. These features strongly suggest that the middle clause should likewise be understood as bearing some reference to time.

But what then is John saying? It is clear that he does not mean by the last two clauses the *same* thing, inasmuch as different Greek words underlie the surface similarity in the English translation above. Furthermore, the *hoti* ('because') suggests that the third clause provides the explanation for how it is that the thought of the middle clause can be so. I would suggest, therefore, following Vos,[2] that what John is saying is this: 'He who comes *after* me was *before me* (in his active involvement as the Yahweh of Old Testament times), and the reason I can say this of him is because he was *eternally before me* as the eternal Yahweh of the Old Testament.'

---

[1]BAGD, *emprosthen*, *A Greek-English Lexicon of the New Testament and Other Early Christian Literature* (Second edition; Chicago: University Press, 1979), 257, f.

[2]See Vos, *Biblical Theology*, 347. Cullmann even argues that the last phrase ('because he was before me') alludes to the 'absolute time of the Prologue'. See his '*ho opisō mou erchomenos*,' in *The Early Church* (London: SCM Press, 1956), 181: 'The proposition introduced by [*hoti*], looking at the matter from the standpoint of absolute chronology, which is that of the prologue, explains this general statement: he is before me because, being at the beginning of all things [*en archē*], the [*ho opisō mou erchomenos*] is [*prōtos*] in an absolute way….' See also Cullmann's *The Christology of the New Testament*, 28.

JOHN'S IDENTIFYING WITNESS: JESUS IS THE PROMISED OLD TESTAMENT MESSIAH (JOHN 3:28)

It is simply farcical in light of the biblical evidence respecting the relation of John to Jesus for Raymond E. Brown, following J. A. T. Robinson,[3] to deny that John perceived his role to be that of Malachi's 'Elijah' but saw himself rather as the *forerunner* of Malachi's Elijah, and thus that he was speaking of *Elijah* when he made these statements in John 1:15, 30. In other words, on this construction, John was saying something on the order of the following: 'Elijah, who comes after me, ranks higher than I, because he was before me.' Brown cleared the way by this interpretation to draw his further conclusion that John (incorrectly, of course) regarded *Jesus* as the Elijah to come who *in turn* would be the forerunner of Yahweh![4] One may easily dispel this view by simply noting that nowhere does John suggest such. To the contrary, he expressly states that he was sent ahead of the Messiah himself: 'You yourselves can testify that I said, "I am not the Messiah but am sent before him"' (John 3:28). Pointing as he ever did to Jesus as the one coming after him it follows that the Baptist believed and taught that Jesus was the promised Messiah.

JOHN'S IDENTIFYING WITNESS: JESUS IS THE SON OF GOD (JOHN 1:34)

After he had baptized Jesus, having seen on that occasion the Spirit's descent like a dove upon Jesus and having heard the Voice from heaven declaring: 'This is my Son, the Beloved; in whom I am well-pleased' (Matt. 3:17; Mark 1:11; Luke 3:22), John testified: 'This is the Son of God' (John 1:34).[5] Many New Testament critical scholars, understanding this title on John's lips as a functional title (what he is *for us*) and not as an ontological title (what he is *in himself* by nature), insist that John was simply saying by it that he regarded Jesus as the Messiah and nothing more. Vos, however, correctly

---

[3] John A. T. Robinson, 'Elijah, John and Jesus,' in *Twelve New Testament Studies* (London: SCM, 1962): 28-52.

[4] Raymond E. Brown, 'Three Quotations from John the Baptist in the Gospel of John,' in *The Catholic Biblical Quarterly* 22 (1960); 297-98; see also his *The Gospel According to John I-XII* (AB) (Garden City, New York: Doubleday, 1966), 64.

[5] The variant readings, mainly Western, 'the Chosen One', 'the Chosen Son', and 'the only Son' do not either singly or collectively have sufficient textual support to overthrow the reading 'the Son', supported as it is by P66, P75, A, B, C, K, L, P, and corrected ℵ. Bruce Metzger, in his *A Textual Commentary on the Greek New Testament*, 200, declares that both the 'age and diversity' of the witnesses support 'the Son' as the best reading.

represents the significance of John's descriptive epithet of Jesus when he writes:

> That [the title 'Son of God'] can not be lower in its import than the same title throughout the Gospel follows from the position it has as the culminating piece of this first stage of witnessing, when compared with the statement of the author of the Gospel (20:31). According to this statement the things recorded of Jesus were written to create belief in the divine sonship of the Saviour. With this in view a series of episodes and discourses have been put in order. Obviously the John-the-Baptist section forms the first in this series, and therein lies the reason, why it issues into the testimony about the Sonship under discussion. That it carried high meaning also appears from [John 1:15, 30], in which nothing less than the preexistence of the Messiah had been already affirmed.[6]

In sum, John intended by this epithet to ascribe nothing short of deity to Jesus, and here accordingly, at the very dawn of the New Age in the forerunner's testimony is the highest conceivable declaration of deity made about him.

JOHN'S IDENTIFYING WITNESS: JESUS IS THE DIVINE BRIDEGROOM (JOHN 3:27-36)

This passage falls into two sections (vv. 27-30 and vv. 31-36), the first of which is clearly the Baptist's testimony, the second being possibly his. In the first, John applies the epithets of 'Bridegroom' to Jesus and 'the friend of the Bridegroom' to himself, adding, 'It is necessary that he [his light (see John 1:7-8; 3:19-21)] increase and I [my light] decrease.' It is only barely conceivable that John's disciples could have heard this reference to the 'bridegroom' and not have been reminded of the Old Testament descriptions of Yahweh as the Bridegroom of Israel (see Isa. 62:5; Hos. 2:2-23; 3:1; Jer. 2:2). It is also only barely possible that John did not intend this comparison to be drawn.

In the second section, which Vos suggests *may* be 'needed to round off the argument of the Baptist on the absurdity of endeavoring to rival Jesus',[7] with which opinion the NASV and the NIV apparently concur as evidenced by their particular placing of quotation marks, Jesus is described as 'the one who comes from above', 'the one who comes from heaven', the one who is 'above all', 'the one whom God sent', 'the one to whom God gave the Spirit

---

[6]Vos, *Biblical Theology*, 351.

[7]Vos, *Biblical Theology*, 352.

without measure', 'the Son whom the Father loves, in whose hands all things have been placed', and the one who brings eternal life to those who believe in him.

In light of all of the Baptist's previous testimony that we have noted respecting Jesus (see again John 1:7, 15, 30; the details surrounding his baptism of Jesus, and Acts 19:4), there is not one single description in this second section that the Baptist could not have given of Jesus. And if it is the Baptist's testimony, then we must conclude that, for him, Jesus was the Christ, the Lord who was to come to his temple, the Messenger of the covenant who was to come, even Yahweh himself who had spoken in Malachi 3:1, and thus the Son of God. It is difficult to conceive of a higher Christology anywhere in Scripture unless it be the Christology of Jesus himself.

Without doubt, the entire relevant biblical witness supports the view then that the Messiah the Baptist envisioned was to be none other than Yahweh himself who was to be 'enfleshed' in the Virgin's womb and who was to come to his temple by means of the Incarnation in the person of Jesus of Nazareth.

JOHN'S IDENTIFYING WITNESS: JESUS IS THE LAMB OF GOD (JOHN 1:29, 36)
John was a remarkable evangelical witness to Christ, identifying Jesus as the Spirit Baptizer (Matt. 3:10-12; Mark 1:7-8; Luke 3:16-17), the Yahweh of the Old Testament (John 1:15, 30), the Messiah (John 3:28), the Son of God (John 1:34), and the Bridegroom (John 3:27-36) in whose hands reside the prerogatives of both salvation and judgment (Matt. 3:10-12). But now we see him identifying Jesus in a striking way that is directly germane to our present study: Pointing his disciples to Jesus he declared: 'Behold the Lamb of God [*ho amnos tou theou*] who bears away the sin of the world!' (John 1:29, 36; *amnos* is also applied to Christ in Acts 8:32, a citation of the LXX version of Isaiah 53:7, and 1 Peter 1:19). It may be a minor point but it must not go unnoticed that John's statement is not merely a comparison by which Jesus is said to be *like* a lamb as in Isaiah 53:7. Rather, John declares that Jesus *is* the Lamb of God. Here the Old Testament's prophesied Lamb, symbolized Lamb, typified Lamb, signified Lamb, codified Lamb, deified Lamb, and personified Lamb is finally identified: He is none other than Jesus of Nazareth! And the genitive of possession ('of God') 'specifically relates Christ to God in the act of sin-bearing. He is at once the sacrificial victim presented to God and the victim provided by God.'[8]

Scholars have pondered much about what specific Old Testament material the Baptist could have had in mind when he made this striking identification,[9] whether the lamb of Genesis 22, the paschal lamb of Exodus 12, the lamb of the daily Levitical sacrifice, the lamb of Isaiah 53, or the 'gentle lamb' of Jeremiah 11:19. C. H. Dodd even suggests that John was alluding to the triumphant warrior lamb of the extra-biblical apocalyptic literature,[10] indicating thereby that Jesus was the Messiah, the king of Israel.[11] In my opinion, since *amnos* occurs in the LXX version of Isaiah 53:7 this Old Testament reference is probably his most immediate source. With pardonable overstatement Franz Delitzsch even declares: 'All the references in the New Testament to the Lamb of God ... spring from this passage in the book of Isaiah.'[12] I think it safer to say that 'all the ideas surrounding the figure of the lamb *built up through the progressive revelation of the OT* may ... go into the concept as it occurs in the NT.'[13] So it is not really necessary that we locate a specific Old Testament verse or passage since eighty-five out of a total of ninety-six passages in the Old Testament, particularly in Exodus, Leviticus, and Numbers, that refer to a lamb speak of the lamb as a sacrifice. Hence, because the Baptist declares that Jesus will 'bear away' [*airōn*] the sin of the world, writes Donald Guthrie: '...whatever its origin, it is indisputable that Jesus is here seen in a vicarious and sacrificial capacity.'[14] Joachim Jeremias, accordingly, affirms:

---

[8]H. D. McDonald, 'Lamb of God,' in *Evangelical Dictionary of Theology*, edited by Walter A. Elwell (Grand Rapids: Baker, 1984), 618.

[9]See D. A. Carson, *The Gospel According to John* (Grand Rapids: Eerdmans, 1991), 149-50, and Leon Morris, *The Gospel According to John* (Grand Rapids: Eerdmans, 1971), 144-8, for helpful surveys of the suggestions that have been put forward. Morris himself affirms that the Apostle John, by his citation of the Baptist, 'is making a general allusion to sacrifice' (147). And we should assume the author of the Gospel would not have used the Baptist's description in a way the Baptist did not intend.

[10]See 1 Enoch 90:9-12; Testament of Joseph 19:8; Testament of Benjamin 3:8.

[11]C. H. Dodd, *The Interpretation of the Fourth Gospel* (Cambridge: University Press, 1953), 230-8.

[12]Franz Delitzsch, *Biblical Commentary on the Prophecies of Isaiah* (Reproduction of third edition in James Martin's translation; Grand Rapids: Eerdmans, n.d.), 323.

[13]McDonald, 'Lamb of God,' in *Evangelical Dictionary of Theology*, 618 (emphasis supplied).

[14]Donald Guthrie, *New Testament Theology* (Downers Grove, Ill., InterVarsity, 1981), 452. It is possible that there is an echo here of the destructive work foretold in Genesis 3:15 in the truth that *Christus Victor* is the one who 'bears away' *all* the sin of the *entire*

...the description of Jesus as *amnos* expresses 1. his patience in suffering (Acts 8:32), 2. his sinlessness (1 Pet. 1:19), and 3. the efficacy of his vicarious death (John 1:29; 1 Pet. 1:19), which like the Passover initiates a new age, brings redemption (from sin), and establishes the people of God (extended now to people of all nations).[15]

I. Howard Marshall concurs: 'The description of Jesus as the Lamb of God belongs to the language of sacrifice....'[16]

In sum, in light of the paschal sacrifice and the protocols of the Old Testament sacrificial system, the Baptist's witness here is a clear allusion, in my opinion, to Jesus' sacrificial death for sin, most immediately drawn, I say again, very likely from Isaiah 53:7. And what is one to do with this sacrificed messianic Lamb? The Baptist 'told the people that they should believe in the one coming after him, that is, in Jesus' (Acts 19:4), that is to say, people should place their trust in him. From all this we see that John the Baptist was a remarkable evangelical witness to Jesus Christ's character and messianic role.

---

world either as the Savior of those who trust him or as the Judge of those who reject him – the Baptist's twofold characterization of the 'one who comes after him' (Matt. 3:10-12). D. A. Carson writes in this connection in *The Gospel According to John*, 150-51:

...the impression gleaned from the Synoptics is that [the Baptist] thought of the Messiah as one who would come in terrible judgments and clean up the sin of Israel. In this light, what John the Baptist meant by 'who takes away the sin of the world' may have had more to do with judgment and destruction than with expiatory sacrifice.

But this does not mean that John the Evangelist limited himself to this understanding of 'Lamb of God' ... it is easy to suppose that the Evangelist understood the Baptist to be [speaking better than he knew].... It is hard to imagine that [the Evangelist] could use an expression such as 'Lamb of God' without thinking of the atoning sacrifice of his resurrected and ascended Saviour ... as a writer who holds that all (Old Testament) Scripture points to Jesus (John 5:39-40), John might well see adequate warrant for the application of this title to Jesus, sacrificially understood, in the lamb of Isaiah 53:7, 10 ... John might also have found warrant for this understanding of the expression in the Passover lamb, and in other Old Testament imagery and institutions.

[15] Joachim Jeremias, *amnos, arēn, arnion*, in Geoffrey Bromiley, *Theological Dictionary of the New Testament* (Abridged in one volume; Grand Rapids: Eerdmans, 1985), 54.

[16] I. Howard Marshall, 'Lamb of God,' in *Dictionary of Jesus and the Gospels*, edited by Joel B. Green, Scot McNight, and I. Howard Marshall (Downers Grove, Ill.: InterVarsity, 1992), 433.

CHAPTER TEN

THE LAMB CRUCIFIED: THE FOUR GOSPELS

The canonical Gospels, while reflecting with respect to genre some characteristics of the popular literature of the time,

> are not fully explainable ... in terms of the Greco-Roman literary setting or by linking them with literary genres of that era. The impetus for the Gospels derives from the religious complexion and needs of early Christianity; and their contents, presuppositions, major themes, and literary texture are heavily influenced by their immediate religious setting as well. In very general terms ... the Gospels can be likened to other examples of Greco-Roman popular biography, but they also form a distinctive group within that broad body of ancient writings.[1]

While all four Gospels are biographical narratives about Jesus that include examples of his deeds and sayings in a loose chronological framework, the sheer amount of narrative each Evangelist devotes to the *last* week of Jesus' life (Matthew eight out of the English version's twenty-eight chapters; Mark six out of its sixteen chapters, Luke five and a half out of its twenty-four chapters, John nine out of its twenty-one chapters) makes it clear that for the Evangelists the suffering and death of Jesus, the Lamb of God, were central to redemptive history.

All four Gospels make it clear that God gave his Lamb to exile among men, to hunger and thirst amid poverty so dire that he had no place to lay his head, to scourging and the crowning with thorns, to the giving of his back to

---

[1] L. W. Hurtado, 'Gospel (Genre),' in *Dictionary of Jesus and the Gospels*, 282.

wicked smiters and his cheeks to those who plucked out his beard. Finally, the Father gave his Lamb up to death on the cross – a type of execution so ignoble and reprehensible that it was reserved for the meanest and lowest criminal types. Roman law even excluded the Roman citizenry from death by crucifixion – and he gave him up to the awful loneliness expressed in 'the strangest utterance that ever ascended from earth to heaven' (Murray), that cry of dereliction: 'My God, my God, why have you forsaken me?' We hesitate to say it, but say it we must: in those hours at Calvary, God the Father in a sense became a sonless Father, and God the Son a fatherless Son – for us men and for our salvation. Oh, wondrous reach of love that God would give his one and only Son as the Lamb of God to the divine abandonment to and to the dread suffering of a Roman cross for us – the last place in the whole wide world where one would look to find his God and expect to find a saving transaction!

All four Gospels also report that the Roman authorities crucified Jesus at the time of the Passover at the instigation of the Jewish religious leaders, and the historical fact of Jesus' crucifixion virtually every religious scholar (with the exception of Islamic scholars) acknowledges.[2] What is not so readily acknowledged, however, is that Christ's crucifixion as the Lamb of God was a work of *sacrifice* for the sins of others. However, John's Gospel describes Jesus as God's Lamb (*amnos*) who 'bears away the sin of the world' (John 1:29, 36), and as we shall see shortly the New Testament letters are replete with this representation.

---

[2]In the Qu'ran, Sura 4, 'Women,' Muhammad denies as a 'monstrous falsehood' that Jesus was crucified. He states: '[The Jews] did not kill him, nor did they crucify him, but they thought they did.' According to Muslim tradition the Jews crucified a man who resembled Jesus, perhaps even Judas. Jesus himself was taken unharmed directly to heaven (see Sura 3, 'The Imrans,' verse 55, and Sura 4, 'Women,' vv. 156-58). This means as well, of course, that Islam denies Jesus' resurrection from the dead. With these denials Muhammad removes from Christianity's core teaching Jesus' cross and resurrection that are central to his substitutionary atonement. In Sura 5, 'The Table,' verse 103, Muhammad teaches that Allah does not demand sacrifices (see also Sura 6, 'Cattle,' v. 164), which means by implication, in opposition to New Testament teaching that apart from the shedding of Christ's blood there is no forgiveness of sin (Heb. 9:22), that he did not demand Jesus' sacrificial death either. What God demands of mankind, according to Muhammad, is *absolute submission or resignation to his will*. The very word 'Islam' means 'submission', and 'Muslim' means 'one who submits' to the will of Allah. But this leaves mankind in a hopeless condition, for mankind is unspeakably sinful with the corporate guilt of original sin (that Muslims deny), incapable of such submission, and unable to save itself.

Because the Christian's ear is more or less accustomed to such language, the assertion that Christ offered himself up to God on the cross as a *sacrifice* may not appear to be significant. But Christ's death as a sacrifice is replete with implications. Since the Old Testament sacrificial system is the obvious background to the Lamb work of Christ as a sacrifice, the Gospel material presupposes, first, the *sinless perfection* of Christ[3] inasmuch as any sacrifice acceptable to God had to be without blemish (Exod. 12:5: *tâmîm*; 1 Pet. 1:19: *amōmou kai aspilou*); second, the *imputation* or transfer of the sinner's sin to Christ on the analogy of the Levitical legislation (Lev. 1:14; 3:2, 8, 13; 4:4, 15, 14, 19, 33; 16:21-22; Num. 8:12; see also Isa. 53:4, 5, 6, 7, 8, 10, 11, 12); third, the resultant *substitution of Christ* in the stead and place of (Matt. 20:28; Mark 10:45), because of (1 Cor. 8:11; 2 Cor. 8:9), for (Matt. 26:28; Rom. 8:3; 1 Pet. 3:18), and in behalf of (Mark 14:24; Luke 22:19, 20; John 6:51; 10:11, 15; Rom. 5:6, 8; 8:32; 14:15; 1 Cor. 11:24; 15:3; 2 Cor. 5:15, 21; Gal. 1:4; 2:20; 3:31; Eph. 5:2, 25; 1 Thess. 5:10; 1 Tim. 2:6; Titus 2:14; Heb. 2:9; 10:12; 1 Pet. 2:21; 3:18; 1 John 3:16) those sinners whose sins had been imputed to him; and fourth, the expiation or cancellation of their imputed sins that necessarily ensued.

These four implications, taken together, justify the conclusion that Christ's death procured the judicial removal or expiation of the sins of those for whom he died. They also mean, because of the principle of substitution necessarily implicit within the scriptural representation of his death as one of sacrifice, that everything else that Christ did in and by his Lamb work — turning away God's wrath (propitiation), removing his hostility (reconciliation), delivering from the law's condemnation and freeing from guilt and the power of sin (redemption) — has necessarily been fully accomplished for those whose sins he bore.

---

[3]See my *A New Systematic Theology of the Christian Faith*, 629-31, for the details.

CHAPTER ELEVEN

THE LAMB CLARIFIED:
THE NEW TESTAMENT LETTERS

THE LAMB'S DEATH AN *OBEDIENT* DEATH

Christ as God's Lamb, Isaiah prophesied, would be 'led like a lamb to the slaughter, and as a sheep before her shearers is silent, so he did not open his mouth' (53:7), this characterization highlighting his submissive obedience to his Father's will for him. The New Testament letters speak *explicitly* of his obedience: (1) 'Through the obedience of the one man the many will be constituted righteous' (Rom. 5:19); (2) 'He humbled himself and became obedient to death' (Phil 2:8); (3) 'He learned obedience through what he suffered' (Heb. 5:8). And they speak *implicitly* of his obedience when (1) they call him God's 'servant' (Phil. 2:7); (2) when they note that his purpose in life was to do his Father's will (Heb. 10:7); and (3) when they bear witness to his sinless life (2 Cor. 5:21; Heb. 4:15; 7:26). So it was as God's *obedient* Lamb that Christ offered himself up once for all as a sacrifice to satisfy divine justice. It was as God's *obedient* Lamb that Christ 'gave himself as a ransom' (1 Tim. 2:6) and 'bore our sins in his own body on the tree' (1 Pet. 2:24). It was as God's *obedient* Lamb that he 'made peace through the blood of his cross' (Col. 1:20).

John Murray captures the character of Christ's obedience by four terms: its inwardness, its progressiveness, its climax, and its dynamic:[1] *inward* in the sense that his obedience always flowed from his willing, joyous yielding up of himself to his Father's will and law; never was it merely artificial and outward, executed mechanically and perfunctorily (Ps. 40:8; Heb. 10:7); *progressive* in

---

[1]John Murray, 'The Obedience of Christ,' in *Collected Writings of John Murray* (Edinburgh: Banner of Truth, 1977), 2:151-57.

the sense that throughout his entire life he moved in perfect obedience to his Father's will from trial to trial with his will becoming ever more resolute in his determination to do his Father's will; *climactic* in the sense that he faced unprecedented trials both in Gethsemane (Matt. 26:36-46; Mark 14:32-42; Luke 22:39-44) and finally in his Lamb work at the cross; *dynamic* in the sense that he learned the obedience essential to the execution of his messianic task from the things he suffered (Heb. 2:10; 5:8); his trials, temptations, deprivations, and mental and physical sufferings became the instruments in his Father's hand by which he was 'perfected' as the Author of salvation, becoming thereby everything he had to be and enduring everything he had to endure in order to bring many sons to glory.

As God's Lamb Christ by his *preceptive* obedience observed all of the Law's prescriptions. By his *penal* obedience he bore all the sanctions imposed by the law against his people due to their disobedience. By the former he made available a perfect righteousness that is imputed to those who put their trust in him (2 Cor. 5:21). By the latter he bore in himself by legal imputation the penalty due to his people for their sin. With grateful praise the Christian adores the Savior for his obedience, for without it there would be no salvation!

THE LAMB'S DEATH A *SACRIFICIAL* DEATH

Jesus' death as the Lamb of God is represented in the New Testament letters as a *sacrifice* (1 Cor. 5:7; Eph. 5:2; Heb. 7:27; 9:23, 26; 10:12), a *sin offering* to God (Eph. 5:2; Heb. 7:27; 9:14, 28; 10:10, 12, 14), and a *penal substitution* (Matt. 20:28; Mark 10:45; 1 Cor. 6:19-20; 7:23; 1 Tim. 2:6; 1 Pet. 1:18-19). Jesus' 'precious blood as a lamb [*amnou*] without blemish and defect' redeemed Christians (1 Pet. 1:19). And as the Lamb (*arnion*) of God Jesus 'with his blood purchased men to God' (Rev. 5:8-9) and in his blood men 'have washed their robes and made them white' (Rev. 7:14). References to his 'blood' – theological shorthand for his *sacrificial* death – are pervasive throughout the New Testament (Acts 20:28; Rom. 3:25; 5:9; Eph. 1:7; 2:12-13; Col. 1:20; Heb. 9:12, 14; 1 Pet. 1:2, 18-19; 1 John 1:7; Rev. 1:5; 5:9-10). His death is also depicted as the work of a high priest who did not offer something or someone else as a sacrifice for our sins but who offered *himself* up as a sacrifice to God (Heb. 7:26-27; 9:11-14). Because of this pervasive testimony John Murray writes: 'It lies on the face of the New Testament that Christ's work is construed as sacrifice.'[2]

The Lamb's death was a *propitiating* sacrifice, a *reconciling* sacrifice, a *redeeming* sacrifice, and a *destroying* sacrifice. I will say something about each of these biblical characterizations of his death.

THE LAMB'S DEATH A *PROPITIATING* SACRIFICE

Presupposing the wrath of God against human sin, Jesus Christ as God's Lamb died as a *propitiating* sacrifice, turning aside God's wrath by taking away the sins of those for whom he died. Four times in the New Testament letters Christ's Lamb work is described by some derivative of the verb *hilaskesthai* that means in essence 'to propitiate' or 'to placate':

- God 'publicly displayed [Christ Jesus] as a sacrifice that *would turn aside his wrath, taking away sin* [*hilastērion*]' (Rom. 3:25).
- Christ 'had to be made like his brothers in every way in order that he might become a merciful and faithful high priest in service to God, that he *might turn aside God's wrath, taking away* [*hilaskesthai*] *the sins of the people*' (Heb. 2:17).
- 'If any sins, we have an Advocate with the Father, Jesus Christ the righteous one, and he is *the sacrifice that turns aside God's wrath, taking away* [*hilasmos*] our sins' (1 John 2:2).
- God 'loved us and sent his Son as a sacrifice that turns asides God's wrath, taking away [*hilasmon*] our sins' (1 John 4:10).

C. H. Dodd has challenged the understanding of this verb as 'placating an angry person', arguing that the meaning intended by this verb is that of simple expiation or the cancellation of sin, and that the 'wrath of God' denotes not a hostile attitude toward sinners on God's part but only 'the inevitable process of cause and effect in a moral universe'.[3] Both Leon Morris[4] and Roger Nicole[5] have pointed out in vigorous critiques of Dodd's argument that he has made two basic errors: (1) his *extrabiblical* evidence is incomplete, and

---

[2]John Murray, *Redemption – Accomplished and Applied* (Grand Rapids: Eerdmans, 1955), 24.

[3]C. H. Dodd, *Hilaskesthai*, Its Cognates, Derivatives and Synonyms, in the Septuagint,' in *Journal of Theological Studies* 32 (1931): 352-60.

[4]Leon Morris, 'The Use of *hilaskesthai*, etc. in Biblical Greek,' in *The Expository Times* 72, no. 8 (1951): 227-33.

[5]Roger R. Nicole, 'C. H. Dodd and the Doctrine of Propitiation,' in *Westminster Theological Journal* 17, no. 2 (1955): 117-57.

(2) he did not pay enough attention to the *biblical* evidence. They both show that Dodd ignored the books of Maccabees and that he passed over the plain fact that the verb means 'placate' in the writings of Josephus and Philo. And they both show that the idea of the wrath of God is 'stubbornly rooted in the Old Testament, where it is referred to 585 times' by no less than twenty different Hebrew words that underscore God's indignation against human sin and evil.[6]

The matter is no different in the New Testament. The occurrences of the verb in Romans 3:25 and 1 John 2:2 will not tolerate Dodd's deconstructed meaning. In the section leading up to Romans 3:25, namely Romans 1:18–3:20, Paul argues not only the case for universal human sin but also directly refers to God's wrath in 1:18; 2:5, 8; and 3:5. Because divine wrath occupies such an important place in the argument leading up to the usage of this verb in Romans 3:25 one is justified in looking for some expression indicative of its cancellation in the process that accomplishes salvation.

In 1 John 2:1 the reference to Jesus as our Advocate before the Father when we sin, specifically in his character as the righteous one, implies that the one before whom he pleads our cause – who represents the triune Godhead – is displeased with us. Accordingly, the description of Jesus that immediately follows in 1 John 2:2 suggests that it is his advocacy before the Father, specifically in his character as our *hilasmos*, that removes that displeasure. But this means that Jesus' advocacy as our *hilasmos*, since its referent is Godward, is propitiatory and not simply expiatory in nature.

One might ask Dodd, 'If this word-group means only expiation, what would be the result for men if Jesus had not expiated their sin? When they die in their sin, would they not face the divine wrath?' Just so, surely! But does this not show that Jesus' Lamb work satisfies divine justice and removes God's wrath, that is, propitiates God, concerning the sins of those for whom Jesus died? It surely seems so! One might also ask Dodd, 'If God's wrath is simply the inevitable process of cause and effect working itself out in a moral universe, since such a process would be impersonal and as such meaningless, what is the meaning of an impersonal process of wrath in a genuinely theistic universe?'

I would conclude that there is no warrant to depart from the traditional understanding of this word-group in the New Testament literature as

---

[6]Leon Morris, 'Propitiation,' in *Evangelical Dictionary of Theology*, edited by Walter A. Elwell (Grand Rapids: Baker, 1984), 888.

denoting placation or propitiation. The evidence at every critical juncture supports the conclusion that, while the basic idea in the word-group is complex, yet 'the averting of anger [by an offering] seems to represent a stubborn substratum of meaning from which all the usages can be naturally explained.'[7]

God's wrath, of course, must not be construed to any degree as capricious, uncontrolled, or irrational fury. Nor is God himself malicious, vindictive, or spiteful. His wrath is simply his instinctive holy indignation and the settled opposition of his holiness to sin. It is his personal revulsion to evil and his personal vigorous opposition to it, his steady, unrelenting, unremitting, and uncompromising antagonism to evil in all its forms and manifestations. Accordingly, above everything else, it is the demand in God himself that his offended holiness and justice when confronted with human sin must react against it by the wrathful outpouring of divine judgment that necessitated the Lamb work of Christ. When Christ died, because of his infinite worth before God the Father who stands as the legal representative of the triune Godhead, he fully satisfied the demands of God's offended holiness and justice. Apart from Christ's Lamb work God could only have continued in an 'unpropitiated' state and sinners would have had to bear the full brunt of God's wrath against them for their sin.

THE LAMB'S DEATH A *RECONCILING* SACRIFICE
Presupposing God's alienation from the sinner, Jesus Christ as God's Lamb died as a *reconciling* sacrifice, removing God's alienation toward us by taking away the cause of that alienation, namely, our sin. This characterization of Christ's Lamb work is securely grounded upon the following four passages in which words from the *-allassō* word-group are employed, the meaning of which words ('to reconcile') is undisputed:

- 'If, when we were enemies, *we were reconciled [katāllagēmen]* to God through the death of his Son, how must more, *having been reconciled [katāllagēntes]*, shall we be saved by his life. And not only this, but also we rejoice in God through our Lord Jesus Christ, through whom now we received the *reconciliation [katāllagēn]*' (Rom. 5:10-11).
- 'If anyone is in Christ, he is a new creation. The old has gone; behold, the new has come. All this is from God who *reconciled*

[7]Leon Morris, *The Apostolic Preaching of the Cross* (London: Tyndale, 1955), 155.

[*katallaxantos*] us to himself through Christ, and gave to us the ministry of *reconciliation* [*katallagēs*]: that God was, in Christ, reconciling [*katallasōn*] a world unto himself, not imputing to them their trespasses, and entrusted to us the message of *reconciliation* [*katallagēs*]. We are therefore ambassadors in Christ's stead, as though God were summoning [men] through us. We implore in Christ's stead: *Be reconciled* [*katallagēte*] to God. God made him who knew no sin to be sin in our stead, in order that we might become the righteousness of God in him' (2 Cor. 5:17-21).

- '[Christ] is our peace, who made both [Jews and Gentiles] one and destroyed the enmity, the dividing wall of hostility, in his flesh, nullifying the law of commandments with its regulations, in order that the two he might create in himself into one new man, making peace [between them], and that *he might reconcile* [*apokatallaxē*] both in one body to God through the cross, slaying the enmity [of God] by it. And having come he preached the good news of peace to you who were afar off and of peace to those who were near' (Eph. 2:14-17).

- 'God was pleased that in him all the fullness [of deity] should dwell, and through him to *reconcile* [*apokatallaxai*] all things unto him(self), making peace through the blood of his cross, through him whether things on earth or things in heaven. And you were once alienated and enemies in your mind because of evil deeds, but now *he has reconciled* [*apokatēllaxen*] you by the body of his flesh through death, to present you holy and unblemished and blameless in his sight' (Col. 1:19-22).

It is acknowledged on all sides that Christ's Lamb work, construed as a reconciling work, presupposed that a state of alienation existed between God and man because of human sin, and that his death removed that alienation or enmity. What is in debate is whether his work removed God's holy alienation relative to man or man's unholy alienation relative to God. Most Reformed expositors have insisted that the English translation of the *-allassō* word-group only apparently supports a manward reference for his reconciling work and that his Lamb work as a reconciling act is to the contrary, as is his propitiating work, to be construed as having a Godward reference. They urge that by atoning for sin, thereby expiating sin in behalf of those for whom he died, Christ removed the ground of God's alienation respecting them, effecting peace with God as the result.[8]

THE LAMB'S DEATH A *REDEEMING* SACRIFICE

Presupposing our slavery or bondage to sin, Jesus Christ as God's Lamb died as a *redeeming* sacrifice by paying the ransom price for the sins of those for whom he died, thereby purchasing them for God. The relevant New Testament word-groups (*lutroō; agorazō*) support this conclusion:

- Jesus opened his mind to men concerning his death as a ransom when he declared that his life would terminate in a self-sacrificing act that would be '*a ransom for many* [*lutron anti pollōn*].' In saying this he made it clear that he viewed his impending death as a sacrificial death offered up as a ransom in the stead of [*anti*] others (Matt. 20:28; Mark 10:45).
- Peter writes: 'You were not *redeemed* [*elutrōthēte*] with perishable things, such as silver and gold ... but with the precious blood of Christ, a lamb without blemish or defect' (1 Pet. 1:19). Contrasted as it is with silver and gold the blood of Christ is clearly construed as a price paid as a ransom.
- John employs the *agorazō* word-group – a commercial term of the marketplace – to teach the same truth, namely, that redemptive deliverance entails a payment price: 'You are worthy ... because you were slain and *bought* [*ēgorasas*] [men] for God with your blood' (Rev. 5:9; see also Rev. 14:3-4).
- The Author of Hebrews by the contrast he draws in the context of ransoming between the blood of goats and calves and Christ's blood, underscores the price-character of Christ's blood: 'He did not enter by means of the blood of goats and calves; but he entered the Most Holy Place once for all by his own blood, obtaining eternal *redemption* [*lutrōsin*]' (Heb. 9:12; see also 9:15).
- Paul employs the *agorazō* word-group in 1 Corinthians 6:19-20: 'You are not your own; for *you were bought with a price* [*ēgorasthēte timēs*].' In 1 Corinthians 7:23 he declares: '*With a price you were bought*

---

[8]See my *A New Systematic Theology of the Christian Faith*, 646-51, for the exegetical evidence supporting the view that Christ's reconciling work on the cross was primarily Godward in its focus.

[*timēs ēgoraasthēte*]: do not become slaves of men.' In Galatians 3:13 he writes: 'Christ *purchased* [*agorazô*] us from the curse of the law, by becoming a curse for us,' and in Galatians 4:4-5 he teaches that God 'sent his Son ... to *purchase* [*agorazō*] those under the law.'

• In 1 Timothy 2:6 Paul taught in concert with Jesus (Mark 10:45) that he 'gave himself as *a ransom for all* [*antilutron hyper pantōn*],' and in Titus 2:14 he declares that Jesus 'gave himself for us in order that *he might redeem* [*lutrōsētai*] us from all wickedness.'

Christ's Lamb work is clearly portrayed in these passages as a ransom price paid to God's offended justice and it is only theological perversity that leads men to deny this fact. Nevertheless, while Arminian theologians acknowledge that Jesus delivered men from sin by his death, they construe Christ's Lamb work purely in terms of deliverance by power, denying that he paid the penalty for sin. Arminian theologian J. Kenneth Grider argues that where there is talk within the ranks of Arminianism that Christ paid the penalty for sin, it should be viewed as a 'spillover from Calvinism':

A spillover from Calvinism into Arminianism has occurred in recent decades. Thus many Arminians whose theology is not very precise say that Christ paid the penalty for our sins. Yet such a view is foreign to Arminianism.... Arminians teach that what Christ did he did for every person; therefore, what he did could not have been to pay the penalty for sin, since no one would then ever go into eternal perdition.[9]

R. W. Lyon, another Arminian theologian, wants nothing to do with a penal substitutionary atonement that entails the payment of a price:

When the ideas of ransom are linked to the saving activity of God, the idea of price is not present.... When the NT ... speaks of ransom with reference to the work of Christ, the idea is not one of transaction, as though a deal is arranged and a price paid. Rather, the focus is on the *power* (1 Cor. 1:18) of the cross to save.[10]

This is an error of tragic proportions. Benjamin Warfield in his day spoke of those who urged this interpretation upon the church as 'assisting at the death bed of a [worthy] word'.[11] John Murray concurs:

---

[9]J. Kenneth Grider, 'Arminianism,' in *Evangelical Dictionary of Theology*, 80.
[10]R. W. Lyon, 'Ransom,' in *Evangelical Dictionary of Theology*, 907-8.

The idea of redemption must not be reduced to the general notion of deliverance. The language of redemption is the language of purchase and more specifically of ransom. And ransom is the securing of a release by the payment of a price.[12]

THE LAMB'S DEATH A *DESTROYING* SACRIFICE

Presupposing the reality of the kingdom of evil and its power over mankind, Jesus Christ as God's Lamb died as a *destroying* sacrifice. As I noted at the outset of this monograph, in my exposition of Genesis 3:15, John Murray observes: 'It is most significant that the work of Christ, which is so central in our Christian faith, is essentially a work of destruction that terminates upon the power and work of Satan. This is not a peripheral or incidental feature of redemption. It is an integral aspect of its accomplishment.'[13] Accordingly, the following ten New Testament passages specifically speak of the confrontation and conflict between Christ – 'the Seed of the woman' – and Satan and his seed and give suggestions as to how it came about that in the very act of Satan's '[mortally] striking his heel', Christ 'crushed his head':

- The demons who possessed two men cried out to Jesus: 'Have you come here to torture us before the appointed time' (Matt. 8:29).
- '…if I drive out demons by the Spirit of God, then the kingdom of God has come upon you. Or again, how can anyone enter a strong man's house [Satan's domain] and carry off his possessions unless he first ties up the strong man [Satan]?' (Matt. 12:28-29).
- 'When a strong man [Satan], fully armed, guards his own house [his domain], his possessions are safe. But when someone stronger [the Seed of the woman] attacks and overpowers him, he takes away the armor in which the man trusted and divides up the spoils' (Luke 11:21-22).
- '…now the prince of this world [Satan] will be driven out' (John 12:31b).
- '…the prince of this world now stands condemned' (John 16:11).

---

[11]Benjamin B. Warfield, 'Redeemer and Redemption,' in *The Person and Work of Christ* (Philadelphia: Presbyterian and Reformed, 1950), 345.

[12]John Murray, *Redemption – Accomplished and Applied* (Grand Rapids: Eerdmans, 1955), 42.

[13]John Murray, 'The Fall of Man,' in *Collected Writings of John Murray*, 2:68.

- 'The God of peace [through the Lamb's work] will soon crush Satan under your feet' (Rom. 16:20).
- 'Then the end will come, when he hands over the [Messianic] kingdom to God the Father after he has destroyed all [Satan's] dominion, authority and power. For he must reign until he has put all his enemies under his feet' (1 Cor. 15:24-25).
- '[God] … having disarmed [Satan's] powers and authorities, he made a public spectacle of them, triumphing over them by the cross' (Col. 2:13c-15).
- 'Since the children have flesh and blood, he too shared in their humanity so that by his death he might destroy him who holds the power of death – that is, the devil' (Heb. 2:14-15).
- 'The reason the Son of God appeared was to destroy the devil's work' (1 John 3:8c).

Beyond controversy these passages make it clear that Christ's Lamb work was and is intended to be a work of destruction and conquest. By it he would prove himself to be Satan's Victor and thus secure for his own their victory over Satan.

* * * * *

The *expiation* of their sins through the obedient sacrifice of himself in their stead, the satisfying of divine justice and thereby the *propitiation* of divine wrath that was against them, the removal of the divine alienation toward them and thereby his *reconciliation* toward them, *redemption* from the curse of the law and the power and fruitlessness of sin, and the *destruction* of the kingdom of evil that held them captives and slaves – these are the accomplishments of Christ's Lamb work in behalf of all those for whom he died. These are the categories that Scripture employs to clarify his Lamb work, each presupposing, as we have seen, a particular exigency that had to be addressed by that work.

CHAPTER TWELVE

THE LAMB GLORIFIED:
JOHN'S REVELATION

John's Revelation brings us to the climax of redemptive revelation's progressive disclosure of the doctrine of the conquering Lamb of God. When one analyzes the 'Revelation of Jesus Christ' (1:1) for its Christology – its nature as 'apocalyptic' being unique within the New Testament corpus itself – one should not be surprised if he finds the Christology contained therein to be more 'marvelous', if not more 'other worldly', than anywhere else in the New Testament. Indeed, this is what one does find. But this is not to suggest that its representation of Christ differs in any essential way from the rest of Holy Scripture. But it must be acknowledged that its Christology is more consistently 'advanced', to use Beasley-Murray's term,[1] in that it portrays Christ almost singularly from the perspective of his state of exaltation. The customary names and titles for Jesus are still present – 'Jesus' (1:9 [twice]; 12:17; 14:12; 17:6; 19:10 [twice]; 20:4; 22:16), 'Christ' (20:4, 6; see also 'his [the Lord's] Christ,' 11:15; 'his [God's] Christ,' 12:10), Jesus Christ' (1:1, 2, 5), 'Lord' (11:8; probably 14:13; see also 'the Lord of lords,' 17:14; 19:16; and 'the Lord's Day,' 1:10), 'Lord Jesus' (22:20, 21), 'a son of man,' meaning 'a man' (1:13; 14:14; see Dan. 7:13-14), 'the Son of God' (once, in 2:18; but see 'my Father,' 2:27; 3:5, 21; and 'his God and Father,' 1:6), and 'the Word of God' (19:13). But by far, *the most common (twenty-eight times), almost personal, 'new' name which the Apostle John, as the Apocalyptist, uses for the glorified Christ is 'the Lamb'* (arnion;[2] 5:6, 8, 12, 13; 6:1, 16; 7:9, 10, 14, 17;

---

[1] G. R. Beasley-Murray, *The Book of Revelation* (London: Oliphants, 1974), 24.

[2] Johannes Gess, 'Lamb,' in *The New International Dictionary of New Testament Theology*, 2:411, notes that *arnion,* originally a diminutive of *arēn,* meaning 'lambkin', no longer

12:11; 13:8; 14:1, 4 [twice], 10; 15:3; 17:14 [twice]; 19:7, 9; 21:9, 14, 22, 23, 27; 22:1, 3), a representation found elsewhere in the New Testament only at John 1:29, 36, and 1 Peter 1:19 (see Acts 8:32) where the word is *amnos*. And what is truly remarkable about this title in the Revelation is the fact that, while 'the Lamb' is identified as 'the Lamb that was slain' (5:6, 9, 12; 13:8), with allusions to his death in such an expression as 'the blood of the Lamb' (7:14; 12:11), and while the term itself, as Warfield notes, always carries the 'implied reference to the actual sacrifice',[3] *never is the one so designated now a figure of meekness in a state or condition of humility*. Beckwith observes:

> [Lamb] is the name given to him in the most august scenes. As the object of the worship offered by the hosts of heaven and earth, chapts. 4-5; as the unveiler of the destinies of the ages, chapts. 5-6; as one enthroned, before whom and to whom the redeemed render the praise of their salvation, 7:9ff.; as the controller of the book of life, 13:8; as the Lord of the hosts on mount Zion, 14:1; as the victor over the hosts of Antichrist, 17:14; as the spouse of the glorified Church, 19:7; as the temple and light of the new Jerusalem, 21:22f.; as the sharer in the throne of God, 22:1, – Christ is called the Lamb. Nowhere in the occurrence of the name is there evident allusion to the figure of *meekness and gentleness* in suffering.[4]

In other words, if Jesus is 'the Lamb' in the Revelation, it is as the 'Lamb *glorified*' that he is depicted. And it is this depiction of Christ as the glorified Lamb that is dominant throughout the Apocalypse.

Of course, he is certainly a *human* Messiah still, as the 'male child' (12:5, 13), the 'Lion of the tribe of Judah' (5:5), and the 'Root and Offspring of David' (5:5; 22:16) who is capable of dying and who did die, but he is by his exaltation the 'Firstborn from the dead' (1:5), and thus the 'Ruler of the kings of the earth' (1:5), indeed, the 'King of kings and Lord of lords' (19:16; see 17:14). And while he is set off over against God in that he is the Son of God (2:18) and the Word of God (19:13), and in the sense that God is his Father (1:6; 2:27; 3:5, 21; 14:1), indeed, even in the sense that God is his God (1:6; 3:2, 12; see 11:15; 12:10) who gives to him both the authority

---

carries diminutive force in either the LXX or the New Testament. See also Joachim Jeremias, '*amnos*, **arēn**, *arnion*' in *TDNT*, I, 340.

[3]Warfield, *The Lord of Glory*, 290.

[4]Isbon T. Beckwith, *The Apocalypse of John* (Reprint; Grand Rapids: Baker, 1967), 315.

to rule (2:27) and the Revelation itself to show to his servants (1:1), *as God's Lamb he is represented as being himself divine.* Beckwith observes again in this connection:

> ...nowhere else are found these wonderful scenes revealing to the eye and ear the majesty of Christ's ascended state, and these numerous utterances expressing in terms applicable to God alone the truth of his divine nature and power. He is seen in the first vision in a form having the semblance of a man, yet glorified with attributes by which the Old Testament writers have sought to portray the glory of God; his hair is white as snow, his face shines with the dazzling light of the sun, his eyes are a flame of fire, his voice as the thunder of many waters; he announces himself as eternal, as one who though he died is the essentially living One, having all power over death, 1:13-18. He appears in the court of heaven as coequal with God in the adoration offered by the highest hosts of heaven and by all the world, 5:6-14. He is seen coming forth on the clouds as the judge and arbiter of the world, 14:14-16. Wearing crowns and insignia which mark him as King of kings and Lord of lords, he leads out the armies of heaven to the great battle with Antichrist, 19:11-21. In keeping with these scenes, attributes and prerogatives understood to belong to God only are assigned to him either alone or as joined with God; he is the Alpha and Omega, the first and the last, the beginning and the end, 22:13, 1:17, 2:8 – a designation which God also utters of himself, 1:8, see Isa. 44:6, 48:12; worship is offered to him in common with God, 7:10, 5:13 – a worship which angelic beings are forbidden to receive, 19:10; doxologies are raised to him as to God, 1:6; the throne of God is his throne, the priests of God are his priests, 3:21, 22:1, 20:6; life belongs essentially to him as to God, compare 1:18 with 4:9, 10.[5]

---

[5]Beckwith, *The Apocalypse of John*, 312-13. In this same regard, H. B. Swete, *The Apocalypse of St John* (Third edition; London: Macmillan, 1911), clxii, writes: 'What is the relation of Christ, in His glorified state, to God? (i) He has the prerogatives of God. He searches men's hearts (2:23); He can kill and restore to life (1:18; 2:23); He receives a worship which is rendered without distinction to God (5:13); His priests are also priests of God (20:6); He occupies one throne with God (22:1, 3), and shares one sovereignty (11:15). (ii) Christ receives the titles of God. He is the Living One (1:18), the Holy and the True (3:7), the Alpha and the Omega, the First and the Last, the Beginning and the End (22:13). (iii) Passages which in the Old Testament relate to God are without hesitation applied to Christ, e.g. Deut. 10:17 (Apoc. 17:14), Prov. 3:12 (Apoc. 3:19), Dan. 7:9 (Apoc. 1:14), Zech. 4:10 (Apoc. 5:6). Thus the writer seems either to coordinate or to identify Christ with God. Yet he is certainly not conscious of

Beasley-Murray likewise affirms:

> Constantly the attributes of God are ascribed to Christ, as in the opening
> vision of the first chapter, which is significantly a vision of Christ and not
> of God. The lineaments of the risen Lord are those of the Ancient of Days
> and of his angel in the book of Daniel (chs. 7 and 10). Christ is confessed
> as Alpha and Omega (22:13), as God is also (1:8). The implications of the
> claim are drawn out in the book as a whole.... In the closing vision of the
> city of God...God and the Lamb are united as Lord of the kingdom and
> source of its blessedness. It is especially noteworthy that John depicts the
> throne of God and the Lamb as the source of the river of water of life in
> the city, thereby conveying the notion of a single throne, a single rule, and a
> single source of life. He adds, 'his servants shall worship him; they shall see
> his face, and his name shall be on their foreheads' (22:3f.). In the context
> it is difficult to interpret the pronoun 'his' as meaning anything other than
> 'God and the Lamb' as a unity. The Lamb remains the mediator..., yet he is
> inseparable from the God who enacts his works ... through him.[6]

In light of these facts, we may bring this overview of the Revelation to a close
by concluding that any reader who will take the time to check for himself
will discover that the Revelation sets before its reader an awe-inspiring
divine Christ under his title as the 'Lamb that was slain' and thus unites its
witness, and that in a singularly marvelous way, to the consentient testimony
of the Bible as a whole in support of both the full and unabridged deity of the
Son of God and his singular work as the Lamb of God.

* * * * *

I have now traced the progressive unfolding of the major revelatory advances
concerning the Lamb of God through both Testaments and have demonstrated
that the 'Lamb that was slain *from* the creation of the world' (Rev. 13:8),
indeed, who 'was chosen *before* the creation of the world' (1 Pet. 1:19-20),
and who would 'take away the sin of the world' (John 1:29), was in the
Old Testament *prophesied* in Genesis 3:15, *symbolized* in Genesis 22:1-14,
typified in Exodus 12:1-13, *foresignified* by the tabernacle and the Aaronic
priesthood, *codified* in Leviticus 1–7 and 16:1-16, *deified* in Isaiah 7:14 and

---

any tendency to ditheism, for his book ... is rigidly monotheistic; nor, on the other hand,
is he guilty of confusing the two Persons.'

[6]Beasley-Murray, *The Book of Revelation*, 24-25. See also Warfield, *The Lord of Glory*,
294-97.

9:6, and *personified* in Isaiah 53:1-12, and in the New Testament *identified* in John 1:29, *crucified* in the Gospels, *clarified* in the New Testament letters, and fully and finally *glorified* in John's Revelation!

This doctrine of the Lamb's work, like no other, clearly demonstrates that 'the New Testament is *latent* in the Old; the Old is *patent* in the New,' that the Old Testament is the shadow while the New Testament is the substance, that the Old Testament is typical and prophetical while the New Testament is antitypical and the fulfillment of the prophetical. This doctrine displays the intrinsic covenantal and redemptive unity of the entirety of Holy Scripture, highlighting the fact that 'the doctrine of redemption was essentially the same for those who lived under the old covenant as it is for the Church of the New Testament.'[7] The Bible's teaching on the place of the Lamb throughout redemptive history shows the unity and continuity of the one covenant of grace, that there is one Savior throughout, that there is one plan of salvation throughout, and that there is one people of God throughout. In concert with the historic Reformed confessions we joyfully sing:

In the cross of Christ I glory,
Towering o'er the wrecks of time;
All the light of sacred story
Gathers round its head sublime.

In sum, Christ, the conquering *Lamb of God*, occupies center stage throughout Holy Scripture from Genesis to the Revelation, indeed, from eternity to eternity. He is the Alpha and Omega, the beginning, the center, and the end of God's eternal will and all his ways and works.

As one reflects upon this topic – central to Holy Scripture – one should be aware that Christ's 'Lamb work' is sacred ground. It is the Church's 'Most Holy Place'. John Murray describes our Lord's 'Lamb work' at Calvary as 'the most solemn spectacle in all history, a spectacle unparalleled, unique, unrepeated, and unrepeatable.' Beholding it,

we are spectators of a wonder the praise and glory of which eternity will not exhaust. It is the Lord of Glory, the Son of God incarnate, the God-man, drinking the cup given him by the eternal Father, the cup of woe and of indescribable agony. We almost hesitate to say so. But it must be said. It is God in our nature forsaken of God.... There is no reproduction or parallel

---

[7]Louis Berkhof, *Principles of Biblical Interpretation* (Grand Rapids: Baker, 1966), 135.

in the experience of archangels or of the greatest saints. The faintest parallel would crush the holiest of men and the mightiest of the angelic host.[8]

The Lamb work of Christ is central not only to the Christian faith but also to its gospel proclamation because of who he was who died on the cross and what it was he accomplished there. The Church affirms that the one who died there as God's Lamb was the eternal Son of God, the Lord of glory, the Word who became flesh, the majesty of whose person and the might of whose power out-rivals the pomp and circumstance of all the petty kings and Caesars of this world. In its best moments the Church has gloried in nothing but his Lamb work (Gal. 5:14) and has resolved to know nothing among the nations except Jesus Christ and him crucified (1 Cor. 2:2). It has done so because it recognizes, as the inspired Apostle declared, that the Lamb work of Christ crucified is 'the power of God and the wisdom of God' (1 Cor. 1:24). Only the Lamb work of Christ crucified expiates sin, propitiates the divine wrath, removes God's alienation toward sinners, redeems sinners from the curse of the Law and the guilt and power and sin, and brings Satan's kingdom to its knees. And only faith in that work makes these salvific benefits the sinner's possession. John Calvin rightly affirmed all this when he wrote:

> ...our whole salvation and all its parts are comprehended in Christ. We should therefore take care not to derive the least portion of it from anywhere else. If we seek salvation, we are taught by the very name of Jesus that it is 'of him.' If we seek any other gifts of the Spirit, they will be found in his anointing. If we seek strength, it lies in his dominion; if purity, in his conception; if gentleness, it appears in his birth. For by his birth he was made like us in all respects that he might learn to feel our pain. If we seek redemption, it lies in his passion; if acquittal, in his condemnation; if remission of the curse, in his cross; if satisfaction, in his sacrifice; if purification, in his blood; if reconciliation, in his descent into hell; if mortification of the flesh, in his tomb; if newness of life, in his resurrection; if immortality, in the same; if inheritance of the Heavenly Kingdom, in his entrance into heaven; if protection, if security, if abundant supply of all blessings, in his Kingdom; if untroubled expectation of judgment, in the power given to him to judge. In short, since rich store of every kind of good abounds in him, let us drink our fill from his fountain, and from no other.[9]

---

[8]John Murray, *Redemption – Accomplished and Applied*, 77-8.

[9]John Calvin, *Institutes of the Christian Religion*, 2.16.19.

CHAPTER THIRTEEN

CONCLUSION

We come now to the all-important question: Why did God the Father go to such lengths to arrange that God the Son, the Second Person of the Godhead, would become incarnate in Jesus Christ as the antitypical Lamb who would take away the sin of the world by being crucified at Calvary? The answer can be put quite simply: He did it to ground the 'good news' of the gospel that alone saves lost and sinful men from the wrath of God, for *without that good news the world is bereft of good news anywhere.*[1] This response calls for additional comment.

WHAT CHRIST'S LAMB WORK PRESUPPOSES

With respect to the Lamb's work grounding the proclamation of the gospel, it must be noted that his work presupposes not only humankind's moral depravity, moral inability, and real guilt before God but also God's judgment of mankind that will someday ensue. The Bible is quite clear that in Adam's *representative* first transgression we *all* sinned and fell with him (Rom. 5:12) – Jews and Gentiles, men and women, rich and poor, young and old. In Adam we sinned against God's holy law and are continually falling short of

---

[1]At the more ultimate decretal level God did all this in order both to 'exalt [the Lamb of God] to the highest place and give him the name that is above every name, that at the name of Jesus every knee should bow in heaven and on earth and under the earth, and every tongue confess that Jesus Christ is Lord' (Phil. 2:9-11) and to make him the 'firstborn among many brothers' (Rom. 8:19). And beyond this, God the Father determined to do this 'to the praise of his glorious grace' (Eph. 1:6) 'in order that in the coming ages he might show the incomparable riches of his grace expressed in his kindness to us in Christ Jesus' (Eph. 2:7).

his glorious righteousness (Rom. 3:23). None of us is righteous, not even one! If one doubts this he should read the Apostle Paul's litany of indictments – fourteen in all – against mankind in general in Romans 3:9-18.

The Word of God also provides a lengthy list of moral 'cannots' that are true of humankind because of their native unrighteousness. For example, the Bible teaches that

- 'a bad tree *cannot bear* good fruit' (Matt. 7:18) and that people are naturally 'bad trees';

- unless a person is born from above, he '*cannot see*' much less '*enter* the kingdom of God' (John 3:3, 5);

- '*no one can come* to Jesus Christ unless the Father draws him' and 'enables him' to come (John 6:44, 45);

- people '*cannot accept* the Spirit of truth [this is what theologians call moral inability], because they neither see him nor know him [this is what theologians call moral depravity]' (John 14:17);

- people *cannot* bear any true moral fruit on their own, for according to Jesus:

- 'No branch can bear fruit by itself; it must remain in the vine. *Neither can you bear fruit unless you remain in me.* I am the vine … apart from me *you can do nothing*' (John 15:4-5);

- 'the sinful mind … *does not submit* to God's law [there it is again, moral depravity]; nor *can it do so* [there it is again, moral inability]. Those controlled by the sinful nature *cannot please* God' (Rom. 8:7 8);

- 'the person without the Spirit *does not accept* the things that come from the Spirit of God, for they are foolishness to him [there it is again, moral depravity], and he *cannot understand* them [there it is again, moral inability], because they are discernable only through the Spirit's enabling' (1 Cor. 2:14);

- '*no one can say*, "Jesus is Lord",' and mean it in the sense that Paul intends it, that is, savingly, 'except by the Holy Spirit' (1 Cor. 12:3);

- people '*cannot [even] tame* their [own] tongues' – bodily organs that are 'restless evils, full of deadly poison' (Jas. 3:8);

- *no one can learn* the 'new song' that is sung around the throne of God except he be redeemed (Rev. 14:3);

- it is as impossible for people to improve their character or act in a way that is distinct from their native corruption as it is for 'the

Ethiopian to change his skin or the leopard to change his spots' (Jer. 13:23).

So in its raw *natural* state the entire human race is incapable of the understanding, the affections, and the will to act that, taken together, would enable it apart from *supernatural* aid coming to it *ab extra* to be subject to the law of God, to respond to the gospel of God, and to love God as people ought.

As a result, in our raw, natural state we are *all* sinners. Our sinful nature is so overpowering and blinding that it can defeat and take captive even the strongest human will among us that would oppose it. Accordingly, we have *all* spurned God's voice and rejected his pleas, we have *all* responded to the overtures of his common grace and of his eternal love for us with enmity and abject obstinacy. Our transgressions of God's law are unmitigatingly inexcusable, utterly indefensible and fully deserve his punishment. Our sin is not only real evil, morally wrong, the violation of God's law, and therefore, detestable, odious, ugly, disgusting, filthy, loathsome, and ought not to be, but it is also the contradiction of God's perfection, cannot but meet with his undiluted disapproval and wrath, and is *damnable* in the strongest sense of the word because it so dreadfully *dishonors* God. God *must* react with holy indignation. He *cannot* do otherwise. And when I say God *cannot* do otherwise,

> we come face to face with a divine 'cannot' that bespeaks not divine weakness but everlasting strength, not reproach but inestimable glory. He cannot deny himself. To be complacent towards that which is the contradiction of his own holiness would be a denial of himself. So that wrath against sin is the correlate of his holiness. And this is just saying that the justice of God demands that sin receive its retribution. The question [to be squarely faced then] is not at all: How can God, being what he is, send men to hell? The question is, How can God, being what he is, save them from hell?[2]

And the only answer is by the Lamb work of Jesus Christ on the basis of which the moment penitent sinners place their faith in him God forgives them of all their sins and imputes both to them personally and to their weak and imperfect 'good works'[3] the moral perfection of the obedience of his

---

[2]John Murray, 'The Nature of Sin,' in *Collected Writings of John Murray* (Edinburgh: Banner of Truth, 1977), 2:81-2.

Lamb, Jesus Christ (see Acts 13:38-39; Gal. 2:16; Rom. 1:16-17; 3:21-22, 28; 4:4-15; 2 Cor. 5:21; Eph. 2:8-10), thereby constituting and declaring them righteous in his sight. The imputed perfect righteousness of the Lamb of God is sufficient in itself to save completely and forever the chief of sinners. As *Westminster Larger Catechism*, Question 73 states:

> Faith [in Christ] justifies a sinner in the sight of God, not because of those other graces which do always accompany it, or of good works that are the fruits of it, nor as if the grace of faith, or any act thereof, were imputed to him for justification, but only as it is an instrument by which he receiveth and applieth Christ and his righteousness.

And those who would intermingle with their faith in Christ and his obedience to any degree their own feeble efforts of obedience as the ground of their final justification before God ignore the Apostle Paul's inspired warning that when they do so they

- stand under apostolic condemnation (Gal. 1:8-9),
- have made Christ's Lamb work of no value to them (Gal. 5:2),
- have alienated themselves from Christ (Gal. 5:4a),
- have set aside (Gal. 2:21) and have fallen away from grace in the sense that they have placed themselves once again under the Law as the way of salvation (Gal. 3:10; 5:4b), and
- have abolished the offense of the cross (Gal. 5:11) because they are trusting in a 'different gospel [from Paul's] that is no gospel at all' (Gal. 1:6-7); indeed, their false 'gospel' requires them to 'continue to do everything written in the Book of the Law' (Gal. 3:10) perfectly as the ground of their justification before God.

JOHN CALVIN ON JUSTIFICATION BY FAITH ALONE AS THE GOSPEL

In the sixteenth century John Calvin termed the doctrine of justification by faith alone in Jesus Christ 'the main hinge on which religion turns' (*Institutes*,

---

[3] *Westminster Confession of Faith*, XVI.5, 6 (emphasis supplied) states: '…as [our best works] are wrought by us, they are defiled, and *mixed with so much weakness and imperfection*, that they cannot endure the severity of God's judgment. Yet notwithstanding, the persons of believers being accepted through Christ, their good works also are accepted in him; not as though they were wholly unblamable and unreprovable in God's sight; but that he, looking upon them in his Son, is pleased to accept and reward that which is sincere, *although accompanied with many weaknesses and imperfections*.'

3.11.1), 'the sum of all piety' (*Institutes*, 3.15.7), and 'the first and keenest subject of controversy' between Rome and the Reformation.[4] Calvin also asserted that 'wherever the knowledge of [this doctrine] is taken away, the glory of Christ is extinguished, religion abolished, the Church destroyed, and the hope of salvation utterly overthrown.'[5] He treats justification by faith alone in his *Institutes*, Book 3, Chapters 11–19, first defining what he means by justification:

- '…he is justified who is reckoned in the condition not of a sinner, but of a righteous man; and for that reason, he stands firm before God's judgment seat while all sinners fall. If an innocent accused person be summoned before the judgment seat of a fair judge, where he will be judged according to his innocence, he is said to be 'justified' before the judge. Thus, justified before God is the man who, freed from the company of sinners, has God to witness and affirm his righteousness' (*Institutes*, 3.11.2);
- '…justified by faith is he who, excluded from the righteousness of works, grasps the righteousness of Christ through faith, and clothed in it, appears in God's sight not as a sinner but as a righteous man' (*Institutes*, 3.11.2).

He then declares that the ground of our justification is Christ's righteousness alone:

- 'Therefore, we explain justification simply as the acceptance with which God receives us into his favor as righteous men. And we say that it consists in the remission of sins and the imputation of Christ's righteousness' (*Institutes*, 3.11.2);
- '…since God justifies us by the intercession of Christ, he absolves us not by the confirmation of our own innocence but by the imputation of righteousness, so that we who are not righteous in ourselves may be reckoned as such in Christ' (*Institutes*, 3.11.3).

He then states:

---

[4]John Calvin, 'Reply to Sadoleto,' in *A Reformation Debate* (Grand Rapids: Baker, 1966), 66.
[5]Calvin, 'Reply to Sadoleto,' 66

...the best passage of all on this matter [2 Cor. 5:18-21] is the one in which [Paul] teaches that the sum of the gospel embassy is to reconcile us to God, since God is willing to receive us into grace through Christ, not counting our sins against us. Let my readers carefully ponder the whole passage. For a little later Paul adds by way of explanation: 'Christ, who was without sin, was made sin for us,' to designate the means of reconciliation. Doubtless he means by the word 'reconciled' nothing but 'justified.' And surely, what he teaches elsewhere – that 'we are made righteous by Christ's obedience' – could not stand unless we are reckoned righteous before God in Christ *and apart from ourselves* (*Institutes*, 3.11.4, emphasis supplied).

Calvin then addresses the error of virtually all of professing Christendom, namely, the 'pernicious hypocrisy' that we obtain right standing before God through faith in Christ plus our own works of righteousness:

- '...a great part of mankind imagine that righteousness is composed of faith and works [but according to Phil. 3:8-9] a man who wishes to obtain Christ's righteousness must abandon his own righteousness.... From this it follows that so long as any particle of works righteousness remains some occasion for boasting remains with us' (*Institutes*, 3.11.13).
- '...according to [the Sophists, that is, the medieval Schoolmen of the Sorbonne, the theological faculty of the University of Paris], man is justified by both faith and works provided they are not his own works but the gifts of Christ and the fruit of regeneration. [But] all works are excluded, whatever title may grace them...' (*Institutes*, 3.11.14).
- '...Scripture, when it speaks of faith righteousness, leads us ... to turn aside from the contemplation of our own works and look solely upon God's mercy and Christ's perfection' (*Institutes*, 3.11.16).
- '[The Sophists] cavil against our doctrine when we say that man is justified by faith alone. They dare not deny that man is justified by faith because it recurs so often in Scripture. But since the word 'alone' is nowhere expressed, they do not allow this addition to be made. Is it so? But what will they reply to these words of Paul where he contends that righteousness cannot be of faith unless it be free? How will a free gift agree with works? With what chicaneries will they elude what he says in another passage, that God's righteousness

is revealed in the gospel? If righteousness is revealed in the gospel, surely no mutilated or half righteousness but a full and perfect righteousness is contained there. The law therefore has no place in it. Not only by a false but an obviously ridiculous shift they insist upon excluding this adjective. Does not he who takes everything from works firmly enough ascribe everything to faith alone? What, I pray, do these expressions mean: "His righteousness has been manifested apart from the law"; and, "Man is freely justified"; and, "Apart from the works of the law?" ' (*Institutes*, 3.11.19)

- 'As we were made sinners by one man's disobedience, so we have been justified by one man's obedience. To declare that by him alone we are accounted righteous, what else is this but to lodge our righteousness in Christ's obedience, because the obedience of Christ is reckoned to us as if it were our own' (*Institutes*, 3.11.23).

Calvin then calls attention to the nature of the Judge and the nature of the Final Judgment in *Institutes*, 3.12 – one of the most powerful and awesome chapters in the entire *Institutes*. We must never forget, Calvin writes, that the doctrine of justification is

concerned with the justice not of a human court but of a heavenly tribunal, lest we measure by our own small measure the integrity of works needed to satisfy the divine judgment. ...there are none who more confidently, and as people say, boisterously chatter over the righteousness of works than they who are monstrously plagued with manifest diseases, or creak with defects beneath the skin.... [God's justice is] so perfect that nothing can be admitted except what is in every part whole and complete and undefiled by any corruption. Such was never found in any man and never will be. In the shady cloisters of the schools anyone can easily and readily prattle about the value of works in justifying men. But when we come before the presence of God we must put away such amusements! For there we deal with a serious matter, and do not engage in frivolous word battles. To this question, I insist, we must apply our minds if we would profitably inquire concerning true righteousness: How shall we reply to the Heavenly Judge when he calls us to account? Let us envisage for ourselves that Judge, not as our minds naturally imagine him, but as he is depicted for us in Scripture: by whose brightness the stars are darkened; by whose strength the mountains are melted; by whose wrath the earth is shaken; whose wisdom catches the wise in their craftiness; beside whose purity all things are defiled; whose righteousness not even the [holy] angels can bear; who makes not the guilty man innocent; whose vengeance when once kindled penetrates to the depths of hell. Let us behold him, I say, sitting in judgment to examine the deeds of men: Who will stand confident before his throne? 'Who ... can dwell with the devouring fire?'... 'Who ... can dwell with everlasting burnings? He who walks righteously and speaks the truth.' But let such a one, whoever he is, come forward. Nay, that response causes no one to come forward. For, on the contrary, a terrible voice resounds: 'If thou, O Lord, shouldst mark iniquities, Lord, who shall stand?' (*Institutes*, 3.12.1)

Calvin then cites Bernard:

Where, in fact, are safe and firm rest and security for the weak but in the Savior's wounds? ...the Lord's compassion is my merit. Obviously, I am not devoid of merit so long as he is not devoid of compassion. But if the mercies of the Lord abound, then equally do I abound in merits. Shall I sing my own righteous acts? O Lord, *I shall remember thy righteousness only, for it is also mine*. Namely, he was made righteousness for me by God.... Why should the church be concerned about merits, since it has in God's purpose a surer reason for glorying? Thus there is no reason why you should ask by what merits we may hope for benefits.... Merit enough it is to know that merits are not enough; but as it is merit enough not to presume upon merits, so to be without merits is enough for judgment. (*Institutes*, 3.12.3, emphasis supplied)

Someday our own consciences, Calvin observes, will bear witness to the truth of the exceeding sinfulness of our works and our inability to contribute to our justification before God by anything we do:

...if the stars, which seem so very bright at night, lose their brilliance in the sight of the sun, what do we think will happen even to the rarest innocence of man when it is compared with God's purity? For it will be a very severe test, which will penetrate to the most hidden thoughts of the heart.... This will compel the lurking and lagging conscience to utter all things that have now even been forgotten.... Outward parade of good works ... will be of no benefit there; purity of will alone will be demanded of us. And therefore hypocrisy shall fall down confounded, even as it now vaunts itself with drunken boldness.... They who do not direct their attention to such a spectacle can, indeed, for the moment pleasantly and peacefully construct a righteousness for themselves, but one that will soon in God's judgment be shaken from them, just as great riches heaped up in a dream vanish upon awakening. But they who seriously, and as in God's sight, will seek after the true rule of righteousness, will certainly find that *all human works, if judged according to their own worth, are nothing but filth and defilement.* And what is commonly reckoned righteousness is before God sheer iniquity; what is adjudged uprightness, pollution; what is accounted glory, ignominy. (*Institutes*, 3.12.4, emphasis supplied)

Calvin continues:

> Let us not be ashamed to descend from this contemplation of divine perfection to look upon ourselves, without flattery and without being affected by blind self-love. For … while man flatters himself on account of the outward mask of righteousness that he wears, the Lord meanwhile weighs in his scales the secret impurity of the heart. Since, therefore, a man is far from being benefited by such flatteries, let us not, to our ruin, willingly delude ourselves. In order that we may rightly examine ourselves, our consciences must necessarily be called before God's judgment seat. For there is need to strip entirely bare in its light the secret places of our depravity, which otherwise are too deeply hidden. Then only will we clearly see the value of these words: 'Man is far from being justified before God, man who is rottenness and a worm,' 'abominable and empty, who drinks iniquity like water.' …the rigor of this examination ought to proceed to the extent of casting us down into complete consternation, and in this way preparing us to receive Christ's grace. (*Institutes*, 3.12.5)

What we need to exhibit before God's judgment seat, Calvin concludes, is true humility, not the insistence of false teachers that in addition to Christ's perfect obedience our imperfect works are necessary for our final justification before God:

> …what way do we have to humble ourselves except that, wholly poor and destitute, we yield to God's mercy. For if we think that we have anything left to ourselves, I do not call it humility. And those who have hitherto joined these two things together – namely, that we must think humbly concerning ourselves before God and must reckon our righteousness to be of some value – *have taught a pernicious hypocrisy….* If you would, according to God's judgment, be exalted with the humble, your heart ought to be wounded with … contrition. If that does not happen, you will be humbled by God's

powerful hand to your shame and disgrace (*Institutes*, 3.12.6, emphasis supplied).

My intention in citing Calvin so extensively is to let him speak to the twenty-first-century world and church[6] as if he were still alive. I trust that I have done that. I trust also that most, if not all, of my readers believe that 'justification

---

[6]The Sanders/Dunn 'New Perspective on Paul' argues that Luther and Calvin at the time of the Reformation misunderstood what Paul taught about justification and so constructed an erroneous and misleading doctrine of justification that Protestantism has unwittingly followed to this day. I reject this 'new perspective' as I do the conclusions of certain teachers that have risen within confessing Reformed communions in the last three decades who, following the errant teaching of Norman Shepherd, do not endorse the doctrine of justification as enunciated by their historic church confessions and, instead of doing the honorable thing and leaving these communions, are corrupting the one true law-free gospel and causing division within their communions with their teaching that the Christian's justification is not by faith alone in the all-sufficient work of Jesus Christ but is rather the eschatological end result of the believer's faithfulness to Christ that includes his imperfect works of obedience – the very error against which Calvin warned his readers. These teachers have rejected the clear Pauline teaching that justification is an act of God's free grace alone by which, the moment a penitent sinner places his faith in Christ, he forgives him of all his sins and imputes to him and to his imperfect works the perfect obedience of his Son Jesus Christ (see Acts 13:38-39; Gal. 2:16; Rom. 1:16-17; 3:21-22, 28; 4:4-15; 2 Cor. 5:21; Eph. 2:8-10), thereby constituting and declaring him righteous in his sight. These teachers, either minimizing or denying altogether the imputation of Christ's active obedience to the believer, teach that justification is not a purely forensic declaration but a transforming activity in which the believer's obedience also plays a significant role in his justification. This corrupted doctrine of justification includes within it the old lie of Satan that Christ's righteousness is not enough in itself to justify and that obedience on the part of the believer is necessary for his full and final justification before God. In order to preserve the doctrinal purity of the church, the Reformed church must raise its voice in protest regarding this downgrade trend within the historic Reformed tradition and remind these errant teachers, as the Apostle Paul declares, that those who would intermingle to any degree the believer's obedience with Christ's obedience as the ground of their final justification before God stand under apostolic condemnation (Gal. 1:8-9), have made Christ's cross-work of no value to them (Gal. 5:2), have alienated themselves from Christ (Gal. 5:4a), have set aside (Gal. 2:21) and have fallen away from grace in the sense that they have placed themselves once again under the Law as the way of salvation (Gal. 3:10; 5:4b), and have abolished the offense of the cross (Gal. 5:11) because they are trusting in a 'different gospel [from Paul's] that is no gospel at all' (Gal. 1:6-7), a 'different gospel' that requires them to 'continue to do everything written in the Book of the Law' (Gal. 3:10) perfectly as the ground of their justification.

is an act of God's free grace, wherein he pardoneth all our sins and accepteth us as righteous in his sight, only for the righteousness of Christ, imputed to us, and received by faith alone' (*Westminster Shorter Catechism*, Question 33). Every other plan of salvation, however well intended, will fail, and those who trust in any other plan will be cast into eternal perdition forever!

The burning question for the sixteenth-century Reformers was *Wie kriege ich einen gnädigen Gott?* ('How can I find a gracious God?), or as Job asks: 'How can a mortal be righteous before God? Though one wish to dispute with him, he could not answer him one time out of a thousand' (Job 9:2-3), or as Bildad phrases it: 'How can a man achieve right standing before God? How can one born of woman be pure? If even ... the stars are not pure in his sight, how much less man, who is but a maggot – a son of man, who is only a worm!' (Job 25:4-6) The church of the Medieval Age had taught for centuries that right standing before God was achieved through the Spirit's work of grace *in* the human heart. More specifically, it taught that men achieve heaven through the sacrament of baptism that removes original sin and regenerates, through inner renewal by works of penance that address post-baptismal sins, and by the grace of sanctification that is never complete in this life, which necessitates that Christians go to purgatory after death to make expiation for their sins. Candor requires that it be said that that church, with its Vatican II deliverances that were intended to bring the church into the twentieth century, is still with us today with no change in its false soteriology[7] from that time to our own, declaring again

---

[7]Roman Catholicism declares, because it holds to the early ecumenical creeds, that it is an orthodox church and should be viewed as such by all. The problem here is that these early creeds (Apostles' Creed, Nicene Creed, Niceno-Constantinopolitan Creed, Definition of Chalcedon, and Athanasian Creed) are not *evangelical* creeds, that is, creeds that explicate soteric matters. They were all framed in the context of the Trinitarian debates in the fourth and fifth centuries and are underdeveloped respecting and virtually silent on matters of soteriology. Herman Bavinck in his *The Doctrine of God*, translated by William Hendriksen (Grand Rapids: Baker, 1951), 285, notes: '...the Reformation has brought to light that not the mere historical belief in the doctrine of the trinity, no matter how pure, is sufficient unto salvation, but only the true heart-born confidence that rests in God himself, who in Christ has revealed himself as the triune God.' That is to say, there is *no* saving value in holding to an orthodox view of God as Trinity if one is at the same time also holding to an unorthodox view of the saving work of the Trinity. Consequently, when the counter-Reformation Council of Trent by its Decrees and Canons rejected the doctrine of justification by faith alone and anathematized those who believe this doctrine, Rome in effect formally declared its own departure and

as recently as its 1994 *Catechism of the Catholic Church* that 'justification is ... the sanctification and renewal of the interior man.' I must conclude that the Roman Catholic Church is the greatest organized enemy of the true gospel of justification by faith alone in Christ's Lamb work alone on the planet today! It is, in a word, anti-Christian to the core.

J. C. RYLE ON JUSTIFICATION BY FAITH ALONE

We should heed the insights of another Calvinistic voice of authority on the gospel significance of the doctrine of justification by faith alone. J. C. Ryle (1816–1900), first Bishop of Liverpool in the Church of England, was a rare man in his day. Preacher of the biblical gospel, champion of Evangelicalism, a Christian of exceptional fortitude with deep insight into Holy Scripture and exceptional writing skills, he zealously believed that 'there is no doctrine about which we ought to be so jealous as justification by faith without the deeds of the law.' In believing so, he was simply following in the train of the great Reformer Martin Luther who declared that this doctrine is 'the head and the cornerstone. It alone begets, nourishes, builds, preserves, and defends the church of God; and without it the church of God cannot exist for one hour' (*Werke*, 30/II, 651); that it is 'the chief article of Christian doctrine' (*Werke*, 40/1, 192); that in the doctrine of justification by faith alone in Christ the Lamb's saving work alone 'all the articles of our faith are comprehended' (*Werke*, 40/1, 441); and that this article of faith is the article of a standing and falling church (*articulus stantis et cadentis ecclesiae*) (*Werke*, 40/3, 352, 3).

Why did Ryle so highly regard and so zealously defend the doctrine of justification by faith alone (*sola fide*) through Christ's Lamb work alone (*solus Christus*)? He did so for the following five reasons:

---

apostasy from the apostolic gospel. Rome has not to this day repudiated Trent; to the contrary, it has time and again reaffirmed Trent. So by no stretch of the imagination are the core beliefs of Roman Catholicism and Reformation theology on the gospel, that is, on the doctrine of justification by faith alone, the same today. They differ radically on the gospel itself, with Roman Catholicism teaching the heresy of justification by faith plus works and Reformation theology teaching the biblical truth of justification by faith alone in Christ's perfect obedience, which justifying faith will always be accompanied, as James 2:14-26 teaches, by good works that form no part of the ground of justification but are 'the fruits and evidence of a true and lively faith' (*Westminster Confession of Faith*, XVI.2).

1. Because the doctrine of justification by faith alone in Christ's Lamb work alone is essentially necessary for any and every man's personal comfort.

'No man on earth is a real child of God, and a saved soul, till he sees and receives salvation by faith in Christ Jesus. No man will ever have solid peace and true assurance, until he embraces with all his heart the doctrine that "we are accounted righteous before God for the merit of our Lord Jesus Christ, by faith, and not for our own works and deservings." One reason … why so many professors … are tossed to and fro, enjoy little comfort, and feel little peace, is their ignorance on this point. They do not see clearly justification by faith without the deeds of the law.'

2. Because the great enemy of souls hates and labors to overthrow the doctrine of justification by faith alone in Christ's Lamb work alone. Satan, he writes, knows that this doctrine

'…turned the world upside down at the first beginning of the gospel, in the days of the apostles. He knows that it turned the world upside down again at the time of the Reformation. He is therefore always tempting men to reject it. He is always trying to seduce churches and ministers to deny or obscure its truth. No wonder that the Council of Trent directed its chief attack against this doctrine and pronounced it accursed and heretical! No wonder that many who think themselves learned … denounce the doctrine as theological jargon and say that all "earnest-minded people" are justified by Christ, whether they have faith or not! The plain truth is that the doctrine is all gall and wormwood to unconverted hearts. It just meets the wants of the awakened soul. But the proud, unhumbled man who knows not his own sin, and sees not his own weakness, cannot receive its truth.'

3. Because the absence of the doctrine of justification by faith alone in Christ's Lamb work alone accounts for half the errors of the Roman Catholic Church:

'The beginning of half the unscriptural doctrines of Popery may be traced up to rejection of justification by faith. No Romish teacher, if he is faithful to his church, can say to the anxious sinner, "Believe on the Lord Jesus Christ, and thou shalt be saved." He cannot do it without additions and explanations, which completely destroy the good news. He dare not give the gospel medicine without adding something which destroys its efficacy and neutralizes its power. Purgatory, penance, priestly absolution, the intercession of saints, the worship of the Virgin, and many other man-made services of Popery, all spring from this source. They are all rotten props to support weary consciences. But they are rendered necessary by this denial of justification by faith.'

4. Because the doctrine of justification by faith alone in Christ's Lamb work alone is absolutely essential to a minister's success among his people:

'Obscurity on this point spoils all. Absence of clear statements about justification will prevent the utmost zeal doing good. There may be much that is pleasing and nice in a minister's sermons – much about Christ and sacramental union with Him, much about self-denial, much about humility, much about charity. But all this will profit little, if his trumpet gives an uncertain sound about justification by faith without the deeds of the law.'

5. Because the doctrine of justification by faith alone in Christ's Lamb work alone is absolutely essential to the prosperity of the church:

'No church is really in a healthy state in which this doctrine is not prominently brought forward. A church may have good forms and regularly ordained ministers, and the sacraments properly administered, but a church will not see conversion of souls going on under its pulpits when this doctrine is not plainly preached. Its schools may be found in every parish. Its ecclesiastical buildings may strike the eye all over the land. But there will be no blessing from God on that church unless justification by faith is proclaimed from its pulpits. Sooner or later the candlestick will be taken away.

'...Why do we so often see a splendid Gothic parish church as empty of worshippers as a barn in July, and a little plain brick building, called a meeting-house, filled to suffocation? Is it that people in general have an abstract dislike to episcopacy.... Not at all! The simple reason is, in the vast majority of cases, that people do not like preaching in which justification by faith is not fully proclaimed. When they cannot hear it in the parish church, they will seek it elsewhere. No doubt there are exceptions. No doubt there are places where a long course of neglect has thoroughly disgusted people with the Church of England, so that they will not even hear truth from ministers. But ... as a general rule, when the parish church is empty and the meeting-house full, it will be found on inquiry that *there is a cause.*

'If these things be so, ... whatever we tolerate, let us never allow any injury to be done to that blessed doctrine – that we are justified by faith without the deeds of the law.

'Let us always beware of any teaching which either directly or indirectly obscures justification by faith. All religious systems which put anything between the heavy-laden sinner and Jesus Christ the Savior, except simple faith, are dangerous and unscriptural. All systems which make out faith to be anything complicated, anything but a simple, childlike dependence – the hand which receives the soul's medicine from the physician – are unsafe and poisonous systems. All systems which cast discredit on the simple Protestant doctrine which broke the power of Rome carry about with them a plague-spot and are dangerous to souls.

'...Whenever we hear teaching which obscures or contradicts justification by faith, we may be sure there is a screw loose somewhere. We should watch against such teaching and be upon our guard. Once let a man get wrong about justification, and he will bid a long farewell to comfort, to peace, to lively hope, to anything like assurance in his Christianity. An error here is a worm at the root.'[8]

WHAT THE BIBLICAL GOSPEL IS

We have heard enough to say that the biblical gospel is the good news that what mankind can never do for itself – namely, achieve right standing with God and thereby escape divine judgment – Jesus Christ as God's Lamb has done by his preceptive and penal obedience[9] for others and that those who place their trust in him will receive his saving benefits. The gospel is by definition 'good news' – good news, as we have seen, that Paul defines precisely in terms of the doctrine of justification by faith alone apart from works of law:

'[The gospel] is the power of God for salvation for everyone who believes, for the Jew first and also for the Greek. For *in it[the gospel] the [imputed] righteousness of God is revealed from faith to faith*, as it is written: "The righteous shall live by faith"' (Rom. 1:16-17).

'We know that a man is not justified by works of law but by faith in Jesus Christ. So we, too, have put our faith in Christ Jesus that we may be justified

---

[8]These five reasons may be found in full in J. C. Ryle, 'The Fallibility of Ministers,' *Knots Untied* (Reprint of tenth edition; Moscow, Idaho: Charles Nolan, 2000), 394-9.

[9]By 'preceptive' obedience that some theologians designate 'active obedience' I refer to Christ's perfect obedience to the Law of God that is imputed to us when we trust in him. By 'penal obedience' that these same theologians designate 'passive obedience' I refer to Christ's obedience in bearing the penalty for *our* disobedience to the Law of God.

by faith in Christ and not by works of law, because by works of law no one will be justified' (Gal. 2:16).

'God was, in Christ, reconciling [*katallasōn*] a world unto himself, not imputing to them their trespasses, and [he] entrusted to us the message of *reconciliation* [*katallagēs*]. We are therefore ambassadors in Christ's stead, as though God were summoning [men] through us. We implore in Christ's stead: *Be reconciled* [*katallagēte*] to God. *God made him who knew no sin to be sin in our stead, in order that we might become the righteousness of God in him*' (2 Cor. 5:17-21).

WHAT THE BIBLICAL GOSPEL IS NOT

It is not 'good news' to be informed that the gospel is 'keeping the golden rule' for this is simply sheer legalism. Neither is it good news to be told that one must keep the law of God in order to be saved for this none can ever do perfectly and again is simply legalism. Nor is it 'good news' to be informed that one must both believe in Christ *and* also keep the law in order to be saved for again the latter none can ever do perfectly and is legalism. In fact, the belief that in addition to faith in Christ one must also keep the law in order to be saved actually makes Christ's work of no effect, alienates one from Christ, and abolishes the offense of the cross. Paul wrote his letter to the Galatians to counteract this very idea. He who so believes, writes Paul, is trusting in 'another gospel that is no gospel at all' (Gal. 1:7). The Romanist variation of this false gospel is that in addition to faith in Christ one must also rely on Mary's pristine righteousness and on the supererogatory righteousness of Rome's thousand other gods and intercessors[10] and on his own meritorious works of righteousness in order to be saved. He who so believes places his soul in eternal peril for such belief is not the 'good news' of the biblical gospel but is rather the old paganism wrapped in a quasi-Christian garb. Such hybrids of the true gospel must be roundly rejected. And they *will* be when one comes to understand

- that the *only* man with whom the infinitely holy God can have *direct* fellowship is the Lamb of God, the perfect Godman and only mediator 'between God

---

[10]Anglican Bishop J. C. Ryle in *Warnings to the Churches* (Reprint; Edinburgh: Banner of Truth, 1992), 158 (emphasis in the original), writes: 'Romanism in perfection is a gigantic system of Church-worship, Sacrament-worship, Mary-worship, saint-worship, image-worship, relic-worship, and priest-worship, – ... it is, in one word, a *huge organized idolatry*.'

and man, the man Christ Jesus' (1 Tim. 2:5), and that it is only as sinful people place their trust in Christ's Lamb work and are thereby regarded by God as 'in Christ' that the triune God can have any fellowship with them;

- that the only way to protect the *solus Christus* ('Christ alone')[11] of salvation is to insist upon the *sola fide* ('faith alone') of justification, and the only way to protect the *sola fide* of justification is to insist upon the *solus Christus* of salvation;

- that saving faith is to be directed to the doing and dying of Christ alone and never and in no sense to the good works or inner experience of the believer or of any other believer;

- that the Christian's righteousness before God today is *in heaven* at the right hand of God in Jesus Christ, and *not on earth* within the believer;

- that the ground of our justification is the vicarious work of Christ *for* us, not the gracious work of the Spirit *in* us;

- that the faith-righteousness of justification is not personal but vicarious, not infused but imputed, not experiential but forensic, not psychological but legal, not our own but a righteousness alien to us, and not earned but graciously given to the penitent sinner through faith in Christ, which repentance and faith are themselves gifts of grace; all which means

- that justification by faith is not to be set off over against justification by works as such but over against justification by *our* works, for justification is indeed grounded in Christ the Lamb's alien preceptive and penal obedience in our stead that we receive by imputation through faith alone.

As I conclude I would urge *all* my readers now to examine themselves with respect to whether they are trusting solely in the preceptive and penal

---

[11]Protestants do not believe in the *solus Christus* of salvation in an exclusive sense because Paul expressly declares that one must believe also in the Father (and by extension in the Holy Spirit) if we would be justified (Rom. 4:5, 23). But it is true that one must trust in Christ's preceptive and penal obedience alone as the ground of justification. Indeed, Protestants are Protestants precisely because they take seriously not only the big words of Scripture such as predestination, sanctification, propitiation, and reconciliation but also the little words as well, specifically, the little word 'one' (*heis*), from which the *solus* in *solus Christus* is derived and which by implication carries along with it the *sola* of *sola gratia* and *sola fide*, that is found in the Pauline phrases: 'the *one* man Jesus Christ' (Rom. 5:15), 'through the *one*, Jesus Christ' (Rom. 5:17), 'through *one* act of righteousness' (Rom. 5:18), 'through the obedience of the *one*' (Rom. 5:19), and 'there is … *one* mediator between God and men, the man Christ Jesus' (1 Tim. 2:5). We add to the obedient work of this *one* man *nothing* – neither our 'works of righteousness' that are as filthy rags (Titus 3:5; see Isa. 64:6) nor the so-called 'pristine righteousness' of Mary nor Catholicism's so-called works of supererogation of its designated saints. We add, in a word, nothing! '*Jesus* paid it all; all to *him* I owe. Sin had left a crimson stain; *he* washed it white as snow.'

obedience of the only righteous One, even Jesus Christ, the Lamb of God, for their forgiveness and their needed righteousness before God. For make no mistake about it: The Day will come, as Calvin reminded us, when all of us will stand naked before God, and in that Great Day of his Assize the issue of in whom or in what we trusted here for our salvation will be all-important. Unable to 'answer him once in a thousand times' all of us in that Day will be stripped of all the things in which we may have placed our confidence in this world. We will stand before the Throne of God in that Day in utter poverty in ourselves – without title, without money, without property, without reputation, without personal prestige, *without meritorious works of our own.* And unless we have been forgiven of our sins by faith alone in Christ's Lamb work and have been enrobed solely in his imputed righteousness, God will consign us to eternal perdition for our sins. In other words, unless we have completely repudiated all of our own self-help efforts at salvation and have totally trusted the Lamb's righteous life and sacrificial death alone for our salvation we will be condemned. For *by no works of righteousness* that we will ever do will we be justified before God (see Titus 3:5). *Our so-called works of righteousness simply will not avail before God!* Christ's perfect obedience alone is our only hope for heaven. The Lamb of God has done enough! We must trust *him* if we would be justified, for it is by faith alone in Christ's obedient doing and dying that sinners are justified freely before the high Tribunal of heaven. And when we trust him we will join in singing:

'Worthy is the Lamb, who was slain,
to receive power and wealth and wisdom
and strength and honor and glory and praise!'
(Rev. 5:12)

Christian Focus Publications
publishes books for all ages

Our mission statement –

STAYING FAITHFUL

In dependence upon God we seek to help make His infallible Word, the Bible, relevant. Our aim is to ensure that the Lord Jesus Christ is presented as the only hope to obtain forgiveness of sin, live a useful life and look forward to heaven with Him.

REACHING OUT

Christ's last command requires us to reach out to our world with His gospel. We seek to help fulfill that by publishing books that point people towards Jesus and help them develop a Christ-like maturity. We aim to equip all levels of readers for life, work, ministry and mission.

Books in our adult range are published in three imprints.

Christian Focus contains popular works including biographies, commentaries, basic doctrine and Christian living. Our children's books are also published in this imprint.

Mentor focuses on books written at a level suitable for Bible College and seminary students, pastors, and other serious readers. The imprint includes commentaries, doctrinal studies, examination of current issues and church history.

Christian Heritage contains classic writings from the past.

Christian Focus Publications, Ltd
Geanies House, Fearn, Ross-shire,
IV20 1TW, Scotland, United Kingdom
info@christianfocus.com

For details of our titles visit us on our website
www.christianfocus.com